The Secret of Happy Parents

The Secret of Happy Parents

How to Stay in Love as a Couple and True to Yourself

Steve and Shaaron Biddulph

Special Note

In the book we use the word 'married' in a specific way; that is, to indicate two people in a committed long-term project of loving and learning. It is not necessary to be legally married to do this (and it is possible to be legally married and not in such a project).

Though the book is primarily written with heterosexual couples in mind, we hope gay and lesbian couples will find it just as useful.

Thorsons
An Imprint of HarperCollins*Publishers*
77–85 Fulham Palace Road,
Hammersmith, London W6 8JB

The website address is: www.thorsonselement.com

and *Thorsons* are trademarks of
HarperCollins*Publishers* Ltd

First published in Australia and New Zealand
as *The Making of Love* by Doubleday 1988
Revised and expanded edition by Doubleday 1999
Published in the UK as *How Love Works* by Thorsons 2000
This edition 2004

3 5 7 9 10 8 6 4 2

© Steve and Shaaron Biddulph

Steve and Shaaron Biddulph assert the moral right
to be identified as the authors of this work

A catalogue record for this book
is available from the British Library

ISBN 0 00 718957 5

Printed and bound in Great Britain by
Creative Print and Design Wales, Ebbw Vale

Contents

It doesn't much matter whether you are a billionaire,
or you work in the corner shop.

It doesn't matter if you are good looking,
educated,
famous, or unknown.

You are here, in this life,
to learn how to love, and that's all.

You have always known this.

Foreword

This book was first written in 1988. We had been about ready to retire it, but kept meeting people in shops or in the street who said this was the book of all our books that really helped them the most. So instead of a dose of euthanasia, the book has been resuscitated, massaged, Viagra'd, and given a major renovation! Its aims are now much clearer, the language is simplified, its methods easier and more powerful.

The book's goal is simple: to help you stay married, and enjoying it. And secondly, to help you raise children with a team approach, to survive the dramas and enjoy the delights that children bring. So instead of becoming a divorce statistic, you can be part of a social revolution: the breakthrough generation that learns to make relationships work.

There's something else you should know. This is NOT a book about COPING with the family or fitting yourself in to make a tame and comfortable marriage. Nor is it about sacrificing yourself to conform to society's wishes. It's about how to turn the situations you are in right now – difficulties with sex, problems with partner communication, the challenges of children – into a fire-of-honesty which will burn away your hang-ups, your limitations, and leave you freer and more fulfilled than you currently might think possible. To have the kind of family life that (at least most of the time) makes you want to laugh out loud, and smile with pleasure for being in such a buzzing hive of human loving, clashing and growing. To break free from the modern madness of hurry-earn-and-spend, and get a life.

In raising a family, you can plumb the mysteries of life itself. There is no hotter furnace, no deeper pool to dive into than that of 'married with kids'. This, ultimately, is a book about self-liberation: how to bring more love into your life, and into the world around you, where it is so desperately needed.

There's something more you need to know. Good relationships take time and work; and anyone who tells you differently is lying. It may take twenty years for you to reach the ecstasy in loving that is possible for you and your partner. It may take years for you and your growing children to really understand each other. But if you follow what this books teaches, you will get glimpses and have moments, almost straightaway, that will let you know you are on the right track.

Love is hard. You will have to struggle to be honest, and risk rejection, over and over and over again. It will not always be comfortable; but it will be real, and the intimacy you build will be indestructible and unforgettable.

Some difficulties are necessary but confusion and loneliness are not among them. Our aim is to take away the confusion, to provide a map and tools for the journey. And to let you know through stories and examples that everywhere others are making the same journey, and their learning can be shared.

If you want your relationship – and your family – to thrive, without compromising your spirit, your heart or your values, then this book is written for you.

We hope you like it.

Steve and Shaaron Biddulph
Summer 1999

1

About Us, About You

About Us

A book is really just someone talking: a very one-sided conversation. Since we are about to 'bend your ear' for a couple of hundred pages, you might well be wondering who we – the authors – are, and what we are like. So let's get the embarrassing part out of the way!

We are very ordinary. Our house is never tidy, we laugh a lot, have been known to shout at the kids, we have fights with each other and lose the keys to the car. Aged in our late forties, we are getting old and funny-looking, and to the horror of our offspring, we don't really care! We have lived together for twenty-five years and been married for the last sixteen of those. Our kids are fifteen and eight – a boy and a girl.

Steve grew up in a caring, but very emotionally constrained and rather isolated migrant family. (You guessed it – he's English!) Shaaron is of Irish-German descent. She was born on the canefields of north Queensland, one of five little girls who, with their parents, had to struggle and work very hard to get by.

We were blue-collar kids who were lucky to grow up in

the sixties when you could get an education, and advance in the world beyond the horizons of your parents. After a fairly bumpy adolescence, Steve trained as a counselling psychologist. Shaaron trained as a nurse and then a social worker. Looking back, the training was of limited value but we made some good friends, and it gave us something to do while we were growing up.

Steve specialized in families and children. Shaaron worked with deaf people, and before that, as a very young nurse, had to tackle the deep water of illness, death and bereavement.

Being thrown in the deep end at a young age turned out to be a plus. Unsure of ourselves but eager to do great deeds, we found that our patients appreciated our honesty in admitting that we didn't know much. Not having much else to offer, we learned by listening very closely to people and looking carefully at every movement and expression, really wanting to understand life through those we were supposed to be helping.

By getting this close to our clients, we began to know and like them, often more than they liked themselves. Sometimes this approach of listening was helpful to the people we worked with. At other times, looking back, we were quite useless. But we never met anyone with whom we didn't eventually feel some sense of a bond. This included 'ordinary' people, who were easy to like, but also people who were violent or criminal, even people who had killed others.

Counselling work is very absorbing. But after a few years we began to wonder if something was going wrong with family life in the late twentieth century. We were meeting hundreds of parents every year who had almost identical problems with their children. And hundreds of reasonable, caring couples who were struggling to keep their marriages alive. And this was just in one medium-sized country town (Launceston, Australia, pop. 62 000). Sometimes after a hard day's work, you felt like calling a public meeting and saying: 'What's going on, guys?' Or to put the question another way: 'Why is family life so hard?'

Does normal mean 'screwed up'?

To answer this question, for ourselves, as well as our clients, we read widely and also began travelling and talking to people in different countries. All through the 1970s and 1980s we travelled to observe childhood and family life, spending time in Calcutta in India, in remote villages in Papua New Guinea, and in modern cities like Singapore, San Francisco, Auckland and Beijing.

When we observed the lives of babies in the slums of Calcutta or in the bush of remote New Britain in the Pacific, we were struck by how contented and happy these babies and their parents often seemed. When we noted the lives of parents and children in childcare centres, schools, or suburban backyards in Australia and the US, we were equally struck by how unhappy they often were. The conclusion was alarming: as society got more materially privileged, childhood actually seemed to get worse, and the experience of parenthood somehow seemed harder.

In the West people had cars, health care, good housing and appliances. Our children did not die of preventable diseases and they got good educations. Yet we were time-poor, isolated, lonely and in competition instead of co-operation with those around us. We had traded our emotional wellbeing for material wellbeing and as a result the average

Western family was in poor emotional health. In fact, it was dying of stress.

The question that arose was obvious: was it possible to have a materially good life AND live in the more joy-filled and connected way of people in more traditional societies?

In 1984 Steve wrote a book called *The Secret of Happy Children*, which espoused a more loving and positive style of parenting, at a time when books were more concerned with 'taming' children (or in other words, getting them to fit in with adults' crazy lives). Quietly and without fanfare, *Secret* became popular all over the world.

The original edition of this book was our second one. Writing it together took many arguments and discussions, and so took a long time! By 1998 we had seven books, published in fifteen languages, in almost two million homes.

These days we are older and with our own children half-raised, we are starting to relax a little and not feel like we are solely responsible for saving the world. We feel ourselves

to be a small part of a large social shift – parents gaining in their sense of worth, men reclaiming their place in the family, childhood becoming less oppressive and more secure.

We feel that the best results come not from frantic activism but from going calmly, thinking deeply and living your beliefs, as well as trying to pass them on. We have continued to work to train counsellors, especially in the healing of trauma and abuse, and to teach parenting skills, especially parenting without violence. We work in a circuit of about six countries where our books are popular and organizations exist which share our goals. We sometimes look at our lives in awe. We have been very lucky, yet we have also had enough hardship and disaster to give us a strong feeling for anyone who is doing it hard. We simply feel that it's great to be alive, to have kids, wonderful friends and to see the sun come up another day.

Can a book be a friend?

Reading a book can be a bit impersonal. When you are sitting down talking with someone face to face, then it's easy to get their measure and to feel empathy with them. We may never meet you in person but we want to convey to you the care that went into this book, and hope it comes through in the pages that follow. We hope that a feeling of connectedness grows as you read on. To feel connected, and to feel special, is every child's – and every person's – birthright.

The toddler stepping out into the spring garden knows that the sun shines just for them. This book was written just for you.

About You

Now let's talk about you! You're probably right in the thick of it all. One day you woke up and you weren't a child any more. You've made choices, made mistakes, made commitments, and most likely made children! You have lines on your face, and bits of you are starting to droop.

Is this your life?

When you're young you have dreams that reach far into the future. But as a parent of young children, your dreams get a little more short-term. During these years, your fondest hope is probably of getting half an hour's break and having a good lie down. A wild fantasy would be reading the newspaper right through or getting to bed with enough energy to make love to the stranger that is your partner. Before you know it, you've got teenagers and all the mental challenges they bring. If you're not careful, life can be what happens to you while you're too busy to make other plans.

Today, as you're reading this, your family life may be going really well. Or you may be going through a difficult patch. If it's the latter, this is hardly surprising: family life is tough and we get very little help. We do not have a tradition in our culture for making marriage work, only for making it endure, which is not the same thing. The saying, 'You make your bed and lie in it' was very big in the mid-twentieth century – hardly an introduction to the craft of love. Its companion saying 'Children should be seen and not heard' was not much of a guide to parenting either!

Because of the poor quality teaching that we get in human relationships, many people find family life to be a disheartening part of their lives. Researchers have found that many people feel more in control and successful at work than at home. Instead of being a harbour of comfort and security, home can be the place where you feel least successful.

PRACTICAL STEP 1:
ACKNOWLEDGE YOUR SUCCESS

If you have been feeling overwhelmed or like a failure at family living then it is time you let yourself off the hook. Before we start to talk about how to make things better, it is vitally important that you recognize how much you are actually succeeding. If you and your kids are alive, and have most of your arms and legs, if no-one is dead or in prison (or even if they are) then you have done millions of things right.

Without discounting the mistakes which you may have made, it's still a fact that you have related, communicated, given and received love, and generally succeeded well beyond your conscious knowledge. One day, this will be evident to you.

We are all pioneers, hacking our way through the wilderness of millennial family living where no generation has gone before. In the past, family relationships were often simply an appearance one kept up. People did not expect intimacy or authentic communication. Rules and clichés governed most interactions. Before World War II, marriage was often something that people endured. From the sixties onwards, everything suddenly was reversed. Marriage became a disposable item, to throw away if it didn't work. Now as we enter the twenty-first century we may become the first generation on a wide scale with the knowledge and skills to make relationships work.

You and your family are part of this breakthrough struggle. Everyone around you is having the same experience. Moreover, nothing you do is wasted. You don't 'fail' if a marriage ends, or a kid gets into trouble. Sometimes these things have to be gone through to get where you are going. As long as you keep going, learning and adapting, you can no more fail or go backwards in life than a tree can ungrow.

If you feel unhappy, guilty, miserable or stuck at a particular time, don't just ignore this feeling. But do realize that you feel bad *because part of you knows that something more is possible.* Pay attention to yearnings, regrets and frustrations because they are all signs of the life force in you, and will actually motivate you to keep you moving on to something better, which you know is there.

A loving life or a lonely life?

An elderly woman we know has lived in a nursing home for many years. Her conversations centre mostly on her own discomforts, her irritations with her fellow inmates. Her life doesn't seem to mean much beyond just waiting. Perhaps living in a nursing home has made her like this. Or perhaps she always was rather self-focused. It is sad, and a bit depressing, to visit her.

When our kids were little they once took their most precious possession – a pet baby wombat – to show this old lady. 'Everest' the wombat (don't ask!) was wrapped in a blanket, in a shopping basket, and perhaps we should have explained more loudly just what was in the package as we sat it on the old lady's knee! At the sight of a furry creature among the folds of the blanket she shrieked and almost threw it across the room. She doesn't much like furry things.

Whatever adventures and passions this old lady once had are now not easy to reach. Her relatives will grieve her passing, but not a lot. They seem to be waiting for the relief of hearing that she has died. This is one kind of old age, one kind of life. Can you imagine what it might be like to grow old like this: out of touch, grouchy, self-obsessed and shut away from life?

It doesn't have to be like this. The bestseller *Tuesdays with Morrie*, by Mitch Albom, tells about an old man, a college teacher, who is dying from a slowly paralysing disease. This old man was so loving and interesting and had built up so many dear friendships, that even though he could barely move or even breathe properly, his house was crowded with people, full of love, and he was 'teaching' to the very last – about life and how to live it. Perhaps you know someone just like this, who as they get older seem to get more full of life; not pushed to the edges. You delight in their company whenever you get the chance.

So it seems there are two ways through life. And when you get old it will become very clear which path you have taken. If you choose to make time for love in your life, then love will come back to you when you are old and in need of it. If you focus in on yourself and your own wants and needs, then you had better save lots of money, 'cos no-one is going to care for you much unless you pay them!

The three big questions

These days no-one really expects, when they die, to rise up above the clouds, queue up at some rhinestone encrusted gates and get a quick resume from a bearded guy in a sheet! But in the second half of life, you do start to ask the big questions, like 'How did I do?' It's a good question, and it gets more urgent over time. In the last hours and seconds of your life, these three questions will be centre stage in your thoughts:

1. Do my children still love me, or even like me?
2. Did my partner (or partners) love me, and do they still?

And lastly, the most important of all,

3. Do I love (or even like) myself?

In the end it will be the answers to these questions that will mean you die in joy, or in desolation. The time to do something about these questions is NOW.

The ingredients of a life well lived

Life can be so busy that you never get to look at the big picture. One way to take back some control is by listing the major dimensions of your life and giving them a check-over.

These dimensions might look something like this:

Marriage/partnership
Parenthood
Self-care and self-expression
Community involvement
Friendships
Meaningful work

These are the six pillars of human life, but you don't need all six of them. You can survive on one. Any two can be quite good fun for a while. You probably need three to be really alive. If you have all six, you're probably overdoing it, and should take a holiday immediately.

PRACTICAL STEP 2: THE 'GET A LIFE' QUESTIONNAIRE

(Why not take a minute to find a pen or pencil, as this simple evaluation may turn out to be the start of a whole new life, and you wouldn't want to miss out just because your kids took all the pens away!)

Please rate yourself from 0 to 5 on the following:

Marriage/partnership You have a lively and dynamic relationship with one person which incorporates affection, sexuality, co-operation, fun, hard work and healthy arguments.

nope, not me   0 1 2 3 4 5   yes, I believe I do!

Parenthood You are involved in raising some children, whom you spend lots of time with and feel a sense of enjoyment and pride in, even though they are constantly challenging your limits and stretching your abilities.

yuk, no I hate kids   0 1 2 3 4 5   yes, tired but loving it

Self-care and self-expression You have space and time to reflect, enjoy yourself, explore interests, breathe in and be yourself.

what, who, me?   0 1 2 3 4 5   yes (deep breath) yes indeed

Community involvement Noticing what a selfish and unjust world we live in, you take on some activities that give service to others, or in some cause which you see as ultimately important to the human race.

Stuff others, I live for   0 1 2 3 4 5   yes, I get a lot out myself and my family   of _____

Friendships Over a long period you have made some really special friends. You find time at least monthly to hang out with these people and at least weekly to talk on the phone, and feel the relaxation of sharing problems, laughs, dreams, projects, and enjoying their partners and children where appropriate.

sorry, don't have time   0 1 2 3 4 5   yes, that's true of me

Meaningful work Paid or voluntary, full or part-time, you support yourself and make a contribution to human life. What matters is whether it has meaning, purpose, and is something you can believe in.

I hate my work   0 1 2 3 4 5   I love my work and believe in what it's about

Interpreting the results should be pretty obvious – you can soon see what's missing. If you want to add up the score: 15 means you are going well; 20, you are probably really happy; 25, you are hyperactive!; 10 means life is a bit neglected; 5 – well, you are still breathing, but not exactly living. You must be tough to still be alive, so use some of that toughness to get some happiness into your life. Time for some changes!

Sadly we can't deal with all these life issues in one book. So from here on we will focus down to points one and two: marriage and relationships, and raising kids. Because 80 per cent of people are in this situation, it's a good place to start.

A life to be proud of

In many cultures a family is a source of pride, but for Westerners our most fervent hope when we go out with our family is usually just to avoid embarrassment! *In our culture we are not encouraged to be proud of our parenthood*

J. WRIGHT

or our children. Think about it for a moment; if your children visit you at your workplace, do you glow with pride or do you wince and try and hide them away? To travel with young children in Australia, England or the US, especially on public transport, is to be in a state of perpetual apology. Yet in Asia, Southern Europe, Africa or Latin America children are a passport to instant friendliness, generosity and compliments.

Family life used to be honoured. In the ancient societies, such as the Vedic culture of India, to cultivate a lifelong erotic and companionable relationship, to lovingly and attentively raise children, to earn a simple livelihood, to prepare food and keep house with art and style, was revered and respected. 'Huh!' you're saying. 'Nobody reveres me much!' You may well have come to feel that family life is ordinary. After all, you are just doing the same as everyone else. It's an easy mistake to make – after all, what's enlightening about rushed meals, Marmite stains on your clothes and sleep deprivation? From nappies to teenage rave parties, it all looks like one big chance to fail. Yet think about this for a moment. Would you rather be rich, powerful, influential, famous or loved? And is being loved something that you would be willing to earn?

Family life *can* be drudgery, but it can also be the making of you as a wonderful human being, and partly this is a matter of your attitude. *Parenting is a profession. Marriage is a consummate art.* So they will take a little time to master. Accept you are a learner like every single other person on the earth. Forget about self-development workshops, growth weekends and improvement courses. Being a parent will teach you assertiveness. You'll get relaxation training (in the guise of fatigue!). You'll acquire communication skills, aerobic exercise, time management, inner-child work, and every other kind of self-development you could ask for, in a twenty-year, non-stop marathon.

The root and the flower

Life has natural priorities which cannot be bypassed. You must start with those things that are fundamental: food, sleep, exercise, time to reflect, the love of those close to you. If the basics are not nurtured, nothing else you do is grounded or, if one continues for long enough down this track, things, literally, become insane ...

We once went to a meeting of a youth refuge committee. The new staff person hired by the committee ran out to the car park to meet us and to say what a rough day he'd had, he hadn't even had time to go to the toilet! During the meeting, he became increasingly defensive and agitated, and later that night was hospitalized with a psychotic episode. Eventually he rested up and got better. Steve couldn't help thinking, that man really should have gone to the toilet!

Everyone today talks about balancing work and family, but it's a misconception. It isn't just about balancing two equal sides – one is the root, the other is the flower. If you don't feed the roots, there won't be many flowers.

Back in 1984 as we sat talking and preparing the first edition of this book, our baby son would often start calling to be picked up. The writing work was engrossing and important to us, but a baby can't help being a baby! We put away the writing, and a child's needs were met.

So! You've chosen the path called family and sometimes it gets hard. You may not have known that it was a pathway to making you a complete human being. You may have thought it was just ordinary. Now you understand that you're climbing the biggest, most glorious mountain there is, it may make both the struggles worthwhile, the view worth slowing down to enjoy, and the delights a little clearer to you.

The chapters that come next will spell out how love works, in couple relationships, and with children. They are arranged to follow the natural life cycle of a family:

2. Understanding early attraction
3. Why we choose one person over any other
4. How to understand and navigate 'commitment'

Then we move on to the deepening relationship questions:

5. What kind of couple are you going to be?
6. How to solve conflicts without compromising yourself
7. The importance of fights and how they break through to new honesty

8. Adding kids to the picture, and how this sets off a new level of self-exploration
9. The sex-romance alliance and how to fuel the fires that will burn you free

The chapter on sex and romance is deliberately placed after that about children – these two ingredients often come easily in courtship, but with a house full of kids they require deliberate cultivation!

And finally ...

10. Advanced lessons: how every event in your life – even the disasters – can open you up to a deeper and more fulfilled life.

THE TWO BATTLES OF MODERN LIFE

The battle for childhood

Today a big battle is raging, perhaps the most important struggle of our time. On one side are economic rationalists, including many in departments of Early Childhood at universities, who believe childhood can be professionalized, streamlined and mass-produced to fit the modern world. On the other side, there are those of us who think that love cannot be bought, or hurried, or squeezed into 'quality time', but must be hard won, eyeball to eyeball, skin to skin, between every parent and every child, over years and years of loving and learning.

The battle is for a loving, timeless, individualized and whole childhood. The danger is that kids become lost in our materialist quest, caught in our competitive madness, homogenized into crèche-raised, insecure yuppie rugrats; the shopping centre fodder of an impersonal and conformist world where you are measured by your designer labels, and love, commitment and sacrifice are forgotten.

The debate about putting young babies into long daycare is an obvious aspect of this, as is the battle for parents – including fathers – to be given family-friendly working hours. Corporations – not governments – run the world now, and 'love', 'community' and 'family' are not often in their vocabulary.

Young parents haven't got the time to BE parents – caught up in a roundabout of earn-and-spend. In the Third World it is even worse: workers sleep at the factory; children become prostitutes to save their families from eviction from their land.

We have to link up our energies and give each other encouragement and ideas. Parent power is gradually rising, with the realization that we have to fight for the right to parent our children and for a society that puts people before profits, community before convenience. It's a battle that starts at home, with the decisions we make, but that is linked to the destiny of the whole human race.

The battle for marriage

There's another battle raging too: the battle to save relationships. Over 40 per cent of marriages end in divorce. Our belief from counselling hundreds of couples is that around 70 per cent of these marriage break-ups are preventable. That is, they are caused by people panicking; not having the skills, the support, or sometimes the maturity, to push on through a layer of difficulty which, if it had been faced, would have led to considerable growth. It has been found that people once separated, usually re-partner, then encounter the very same difficulties four or five years down the track – plus all the stresses left over from the first marriage: access, support, and so on. The idea that 'If I could just find the right partner everything would be wonderful', while certainly good to pursue as an ideal, is often flawed because it's the same us that we take wherever we go!

Separated people frequently admit – in the privacy of the counselling room – 'If I knew what I know now, I would have stayed and worked on my marriage'. While there are partners whom are worth leaving: intractably violent, patently untrustworthy, abusive or addicted; the great majority of us marry people with hang-ups very similar to our own, and from whom we could learn a great deal if we were to persist. This doesn't mean putting up with what you don't like, but learning how to negotiate change.

Whoever you are partnered with, it's still the same task. To thrive in love means learning some skills – which this book will help you with. It means putting a priority on having healthy relationships. This means not getting caught up in the pressure of an insane society – the rush to earn and spend – but realizing that time is the most precious commodity in life and investing it in ways that will maximize the love in your life. This might actually mean increasing your own reflective time (sometimes the best thing you can do for your marriage or your family is take a long walk in the countryside – by yourself). And of course increasing the time you spend with each other, to give love the chance to grow.

Time is the central issue of modern life. We no longer walk down grassy lanes to visit our friends, or work in the fields with lots of time to think, so we have to deliberately set aside soul time: time for peaceful reflection; the opportunities for deep and wandering conversations which were once an everyday part of human life. The enemy of love in the modern world is not hate, but hurry. The good news is that whenever we invest time and effort between any two human beings, parent and child, friend and friend, then love will grow.

So these two battles – for more loving lives for children; and more committed, resilient and erotically charged relationships between men and women – are entwined. Our kids don't need us to stay stuck in bad marriages or to leave our difficult marriages behind but to get in and sort out our problems so they can see their parents in a living, yet secure and strengthening union. We owe this stability to ourselves and to them.

To assert the importance of love and people is to hold a bright flaming sword up in the snarling face of economic rationalism, the cancerous culture of get-and-spend. More and more people are doing this. More and more people are choosing love as the central principle of their life. It is important to make this choice and let it be the heart of every action.

2

Compatibility: The Ways We Connect

She:	We just never agree about anything ... kids, money, jobs, where to live, what to do.
He:	That's not true!
She:	See!
We: (laughing)	So how did you two get together?
He: (sits back and smiles)	We ... eell. That's another story!
We:	Tell us about that ...

Three Kinds of Attraction: Liking, Loving and Lust

The family cycle begins, naturally enough, with 'boy meets girl'. It's the attraction of opposites that sparks the explosion that kicks along the whole wheel of life. But attraction is a complicated thing. It has many levels to it, and understanding these levels is vital to a happy love life.

Not everyone gets together in the same way. For instance, some couples are first attracted at the mind level – liking the other person's ideas, finding him or her funny, interesting, stimulating. Other couples may find that they connect initially from the heart level; that warm affection and loving feelings arise easily between them. And of course many couples begin with an obvious sexual attraction, that tantalizing tingling excitement that is pure lust! To complicate it more, the way you feel about the other person is not always mirror-reflected – you can *lust* after someone who only *likes* you, or *love* someone who is only capable of *lust*, and so on. It can be tricky, especially when you are young and inexperienced (or, for that matter, old and stupid).

Levels of attraction are especially important to be aware of in the early stages of finding and choosing a partner. It's important, especially for teenagers, to distinguish these three levels of need and, in handling personal relationships, to be honest with yourself about which is what. Knowing yourself well enough to tell love from lust, liking from loving, is the real sex education and can help avoid countless problems.

It's tough being young, and some lessons can only be learned by experience. Remember in your youth, finally getting up the courage to declare your love to the girl (or boy) of your dreams? Having had some friendliness from them in the past, there seems every reason to hope ... and so you finally take the plunge and pour out your heart! To your horror, they look alarmed and utter those fateful words: 'Oh no ... oh wow ... look ... I really like you, but ...' It's lucky that hope springs eternal, or we'd all be celibate!

Whatever kind of attraction you start with, a developing couple partnership will usually grow to involve all three. When *liking, loving* and *lusting* are present in symphony, then the effect is unforgettable. Since this often happens more by accident in the early years, you will sometimes be left gasping, wondering what you did right! As you get older, you will have to be your own fairy godmother. You will learn more about how to achieve the sustained and deeper communication, so that your love isn't a lucky accident, but an achievement, a deepening well of experiences shared and lessons learned, that you can draw on at any time.

Now let's explore how the three levels of attraction work, and then what to do when they stop working. Even if you've been married for fifty years, you'll enjoy reading this part, to reminisce and understand the journey you have already made. If you're a little younger than that, it might even help you to power your love-life along!

Liking: a meeting of minds

Liking is the safest, easiest kind of human attraction. You can like all kinds and all ages and sexes of people – you can even like people you don't approve of, or would never buy a used car from. Often you will like some things about a person, and dislike other parts of them. (If you like everything about someone, stick around; something you won't like is bound to show up.)

As you get more involved with a person, either as a friend or as a lover, then you might ask them to change behaviour you don't like. Relationships involve changing ourselves all the time. It's no big deal: if you are giving

J.WRIGHT

your lover a back rub, you might do it vigorously, because that's what *you* enjoy. They explain they like a gentler massage, and so you change. If you live together, you might like to make the kitchen spotlessly clean and tidy after every meal. They might prefer to leave the dishes for a big once-a-week cleanup. Committed partners sometimes make big requests of their partner: to give up drinking or smoking or living a life of crime, for instance! Our partners may change, or they may not. We are all aiming to get more of what we like, and less of what we don't.

A trap with liking, especially when we are starting out in a relationship, is that *we will tend to like people just because they like us.* Especially if we are inexperienced or, let's face it, a bit desperate. In fact, it might be their liking us that is the main attraction. If their enthusiasm for our wonderful qualities fades, as well it might, then we might discover we do not like them after all.

In courtship and dating behaviour there is usually a huge amount of talking going on, hours on the phone and late into the night. But it isn't just small talk; it carries all kinds of hidden meanings. 'Do they like me?' 'Do they want to know me better?' 'She yawned – what did she mean by that?' It's a beautiful if rather anxious time, and one which we will remember all our life. Spoken words seem to acquire a powerful magic.

The jokes, repartee, questions and proclamations of what we believe in and what we like and dislike, are part of a natural screening process. We are 'interviewing' for the job of lifetime lover. It's important to find out if this person, who looks great on the surface, is really a horrible psychopath, or hopelessly screwed up, or is exactly your kind of person!

What to look for

What human beings like in another person is pretty universal. Are they kind – to us, and to other people? (How do they treat their mother?) Are they funny – not the try-hard, jokester kind of funny, but good humoured about life, including its difficulties. (Why do the singles columns always have SOH – sense of humour – along with 'likes romantic walks, candlelight dinners', etc. Do they really mean: 'Has to be able to put up with me being a drunk, losing the family car in a card game?' You can just imagine the conversation six months down the track: ' So I burnt the house down – where's your Sense Of Humour?' While we're on the subject, why do the singles ads never say 'Good at washing up' or 'Excellent with crying babies'? And how about those that say 'Children not a problem'? Who are they kidding? But we digress.)

Are they realistic, clear-headed, practical? These are likeable qualities, and very valuable in a partner-to-be. Do they have beliefs and values that you admire, and are they doing something more than just spouting words about these things?

There are other qualities we like too, of course, that are not quite so deep. Lots of people marry or move in with someone because they like their hair, or those cute dimples, or that heaving bosom, or their country music collection. Good luck to them.

A note of caution. Our hormones can be our worst enemy at this stage. From the mid-teens on, nature wants us in love and breeding fast, so a certain amount of applying the brakes is needed. You make the best choices when you are not in such a hurry. That's why it's a good idea at any age to fill up your need to like and be liked with friendships of many kinds, before you get into the tangle of involving yourself in a couple. Loneliness blurs your judgement – believe it.

Loving: the heart connection

Liking usually comes first, but loving can soon follow, and everyone over the age of ten knows that this is a different and more powerful emotion. It's the feeling that says 'special'. Limited edition. Limit one per customer.

Love requires a certain kind of openness and trust, a willingness to be vulnerable. Listen in on this conversation between a couple in their thirties, just beginning a relation-ship, and tentatively beginning to risk being open:

She:	I've been missing you. You haven't called all week!
He:	I wanted to call. After last time, I didn't think you wanted to see me!
She:	But I thought you knew how much I felt for you.
He:	Well . . . you get so critical and cold sometimes.
She:	I . . . I just don't like to feel controlled, that's all.
He:	I don't want to control you.
She:	I know you don't, it's just, well, I'm anxious about being too close to a man again, I don't seem to choose men well.
He:	Thanks very much!
She:	Oh, you know what I mean!

Notice how misunderstanding and hurt can easily arise. Yet only by being honest by saying those risky things like 'I wanted to call' and 'I thought you knew how much I felt for you' can we allow love to grow.

Loving is complex because it carries the baggage and expectations from earlier love experiences, including those from childhood. In men this might include feelings about mothers who were or were not there for us. In women it will tap into memories of fathers who were kind, or mean, attentive, or absent. You might feel a strong attraction to someone who is actually a bastard, because bastards were the people who loved you when you were a child. (More of this later, we're trying to stay positive here.)

Also *strength* of love does not always mean the same as *depth*. You can fall passionately in love with the *idea* of a person, when they are actually quite different. Tricky.

J. WRIGHT

Love can be expressed in words, but it is not about words. The human heart aches, it sings and it soars, but it doesn't talk much! Loving actually causes alarm in some people because it is part of a domain that is unfamiliar – the domain of emotion. Don't panic – feelings are simple!

With increasing honesty as you voice your feelings, a couple can begin to understand and clear up the obstacles to closeness one by one. Love grows through the vulnerability you show, as well as the strength of feelings you admit to. Your real self comes out more and more – and guess what? They still like you! You begin to feel that you can say anything, discuss anything, be completely yourself. It's a great feeling. (Though there's always something new, dark and murky arising from deep down, to make you start all over again.)

The good news is that love between two people may take decades to reach its fullest peak, so you have plenty to look forward to.

So in a growing relationship, men and women find attraction growing from head to head, and also from heart to heart. But there's another level too, so let's rock on down to the basement.

Lust: The fire down below

Sexual attraction is a lifelong, powerful tide which either adds energy and magnetism to relationships, or constantly blasts us apart, depending on our skill and awareness in navigating it. You will often hear sex denigrated as the 'animal' part of our make-up, a Stone Age leftover which disturbs our rational mind. In fact human beings are more dedicatedly and enduringly sexual than any other animal species. (With the possible exception of pygmy chimpanzees, who make us look positively inhibited. But this is a family book, so we won't go into detail.)

In human beings, the original purpose of the sex drive – to motivate reproduction – has been partly diverted to serve an equally important role, that of social connection. Although sex often seems to be a disrupting influence on our social fabric, it is nonetheless the force that creates and holds families and therefore communities together. Obligation and duty wear thin very quickly; they are recent and advanced concepts in evolution: nature counts on much stronger glues to cement us. Our biology has ensured that we will not rely on abstract ideas of loyalty and love, but that commitment will be deeply felt, that these feelings will give us more pleasure and reward than any other path in the long run. Therefore sex, love, communication and long-term bonding are all deeply intertwined in human beings. We make love with our brains, which is why sex is so special and important – and difficult.

Sex and bonding

Let's explore the subject of sexual bonding in more depth. Our sexuality is much more than a simple animal urge to procreate, it is connected to our emotions and our thoughts, and has a magnetic way of drawing people into relationships which can then develop far beyond simply lusty desire. In this way it builds between two people an accumulating reserve of pleasure, security, release and openness.

Lifelong pair-bonds are common in the animal world (and so is promiscuity, but few species combine the two). The unique nature of human sexuality – the intense female orgasm which only humans seem to experience and the absence of the distinct 'on heat' cycle experienced by other mammals – means that (for reasons we do not yet understand) sex is constantly present in our social lives. In evolutionary terms, pair-bonding meant that the whole fabric of family and clan was made more secure and trustworthy. People could spend time away hunting, children could be raised in relative safety, because the sexually forged bond between partner-parents meant that they would yearn for the specific company of that one person, above any other.

This carries a risk though. Put in simple terms, if you have sex with someone, you are very likely to fall in love with them. So clearly, it is not a good idea to get bonded to someone whom your heart and head have huge reservations about. This is why all human cultures are very careful about adolescent sexuality, and why young people themselves, in spite of what adults believe, are actually very conscious about relinquishing their virginity. Research has shown that a surprising 25 per cent of all young people are still virgins at twenty-one. Given the power of sexual attraction, young people have to be admired: most manage to hold out for a relationship with some closeness and mutual vulnerability. Those of us who don't quite manage usually learn the lesson and quickly become more selective.

When 'the fire down below' connects with mental sparkle up top and the glow of emotion from the heart, then all three are charged and magnified. It's worth waiting for.

Compatibility problems: why men and women sometimes miss

Julie Henderson, the bioenergetic therapist who taught us these levels of connection, says that men traditionally have 'closed' (shielded, unresponsive) hearts and 'open' (active, energised) genitals, while women traditionally have 'closed' genitals and 'open' hearts.

Men of the older, stiff-upper-lip generation, would often experience some alarm at the powerful and unsettling emotions that arise, whether it be through falling in love, being present at a birth of a child or saying goodbye to someone forever. In short, these men needed to gain the softening that comes from an open heart.

Older women usually experienced loving feelings as a matter of course, but were often stunned and delighted at

J. WRIGHT

the energetic glow and sense of satisfaction that accompanied their first really good sexual experiences. In short, these women needed to gain the power that comes from 'owning' your pelvis, considered in both ancient yoga and modern bioenergetics to be the energy source of assertiveness and will.

As men became more 'feelingful', and women more assured, healthy and strong contact between the genders became a possibility. Some great marriages emerged in the latter part of the twentieth century. In fact, you can be sure that some couples have always forged equal relationships through sheer strength of character – in biblical times, in Shakespeare's time and in every epoch. The difference in the late twentieth century was that the culture began to support this as a general principle.

Things were looking great – except that the pendulum just kept on swinging!

The trouble with 'New Women' and 'New Men'

The culture of the 1980s and 1990s has produced many tough-hearted women and many more soft-hearted men. This does create a new set of problems from those who gained experience in earlier times.

For years women complained about the pushiness of males, saying they were domineering, insensitive, and so on. Fair enough. But a different kind of complaint has arisen in recent years. Many of today's men have been so filled with the need to be considerate and supportive that they back off from the really lustful pursuit and assertiveness that characterizes spirited sexuality.

We talk with many young women these days who are frustrated by the wimpishness of their men, in bed and out, even though this kind of softer man was what women for a time thought they wanted. Sensitive, yes, but uncertain and childlike, no!

You can be lustfully pleasure-seeking, and also considerate and aware. You can give pleasure fiercely, and take it fiercely. It's a matter of communication, trust, and letting each other know what is wanted and not wanted, without offence. It takes time to develop this. Sometimes decades. When the conditions are right, most women, and most men, find unbridled passion extremely pleasing.

PRACTICAL STEP 3: CAN YOU HAVE SEX TOO SOON?

How soon in a relationship should one hop into bed with one's new love? Ideas on this have swung wildly in the last forty years. People used to wait for years. Today sex on a first date is not uncommon among older single adults.

Mary Pipher in her excellent book *Reviving Ophelia* points out that girls as young as their mid-teens today feel they have to be sexually active; that the sexual revolution has just turned into another pressure. Boys also admit privately that they want more romance and closeness, that sex is a pressure they feel they have to live up to. This is not to say that girls or boys are not also strongly sexually motivated as well. Just that their sense of timing and romance is being violated by what they think is expected of them. It's far from rare for a teenage boy and a girl to have sex because each thinks the other expects it of them.

It's possible that having sex too soon actually prevents closeness, rather than promotes it. Our counselling experience is that many singles get trapped in this pattern, actually preventing any strong or good relationship from growing. One night stands are full of guardedness and morning-after embarrassment. As the veteran family therapist Carl Whitaker once said, it's a penis and a vagina going out on a date together. When you are physically intimate but still mentally distant, you put on more armour. It's a very schizophrenic situation. Like someone who tells their life story to everyone they meet, there is no feeling of specialness or vulnerability. Also, because tension has not had a chance to build, there is no big deal, and the sexual chemistry is only mediocre.

The best sexual bonding requires some tension and exploration, some chasing and holding back, and even some old fashioned courtship. Jumping into lust can fool your senses: you can be confused about whether true liking or loving are present. (What actor Robin Williams calls the difference between Miss Right and Miss Right Now!) Liking actually arises from good AND bad experiences: discovering how your partner reacts when the car breaks down, when you are sick, broke or hassled. These things test the liking and loving you have felt. A hundred hot nights of passion, delightful as they may be, aren't actually going to test any of these things. Lust-based relationships in the real world wind down quite quickly when the other two elements are not around.

The more complete the combination of love, liking and lust, the greater the degree of emotional letting-go into truly transforming sexuality.

Casual sex

The free love ethic of the sixties was to have casual sex with anyone who appealed to you at the time and 'as long as you're honest' everything would be cool. It may have been an important and necessary step when the old order was being overthrown in terms of rigid sex roles, militarism, conformity, and trusting government and business. The sexual revolution moved things along at a great pace.

Before long, however, the fallout started. Casual sex was okay in theory but for most of us it didn't seem to work. Backyard abortions, broken hearts, drugs to block out the pain, and a deadly sense of disillusionment were often the results.

Bodies are not compartmentalized. Your heart, your mind, and your sexuality, are all parts of the whole you. It is not possible to have sex with someone you don't like, don't trust or don't understand, without making enormous internal divisions, shutting down natural energies and emotions.

J. WRIGHT

You can't make love from the waist down, and keep your heart and your head out of the equation, without a lot of personal pain.

Luckily experience is a great teacher. A friend of ours separated from her husband after twelve years of marriage. She went through a rapid series of lovers – perhaps to reassure herself that she was lovable, or to capture the adolescence she felt she had missed. Then one day she told us of a new man. She proudly told us 'I am not going to sleep with him just yet. I think this relationship is the one I really want, and I am going to do it properly'.

Junk sex

Junk food is quick, easy and looks better than it tastes. Just as quality cooking takes time and care, quality loving means getting to know your partner as a person. Junk sex, like junk food, leaves you malnourished. Junk sex is not limited to singles either – many long-standing couples have given up on nourishment and just settle for a diet of relationship pizza.

Putting It Altogether

The phrase 'making love' has come about because it describes so poetically an ideal we all seek. When you get sexuality right, making love is exactly what you are doing. It's not the same as just fucking (though it includes the vigour and earthiness of this lovely Anglo Saxon term). Nor is it the rather fey-sounding 'bonking' of the postmodern gender neutral generation. Your heart opens (softens and beats more powerfully), your genitals open (moisten and enlarge), your mind opens (sharpens and sparkles), to let the other person in at every level. Achieving this is rarely rapid, and can never be a passing thing.

Once you have made LOVE, then just 'having sex' will never do. Teenagers 'fall in' love; adults 'make' love. It is a flame which a skilful human being learns to kindle. In a day-to-day relationship the flame flickers, dies down and flares up again, as we learn to tend it skilfully. Our efforts are rewarded. *Love starts as a blessing, even a fluke, but it continues as an achievement.*

PRACTICAL STEP 4: REMEMBER YOUR FRIENDS

In the excitement of becoming a couple, people make a serious mistake: they forget about their friends. The role of friends in making life happier and easier has been badly neglected in our culture – especially amongst men. Friendships are often seen as almost a casual thing, people to fill in time with until one finds one's 'true love'. The post-war nuclear family was supposed to be totally self-sufficient. Friends were for chatting to at barbecues, to sell Tupperware to, and have over for a game of bridge. Then we began to discover the dramatic fact that the couple or the family in isolation does not work. A family on its own is about as stable as a tent with no pegs. The steep rise in both marriage break-ups and single parenthood soon led people to realize that friends were like insurance – they would be there when marriage failed or was just in a stuck spot. Lack of friends may even cause a marriage break up: it places too much strain on couples and leaves too few support networks in the event of hardship, illness, the death of a child. Today this tide is changing. People are valuing friends more. Men, and women, meet in cafes to chat once a week. The rise of men's groups, and the willingness of parents of young children to build strong and intimate friendships with their neighbours, has begun putting some 'village' back into our lives.

Friends help you to continue to grow as an individual – not just one half of a couple. Long-term friends remember the teenager you once were, what you've loved, lost, tried, and achieved. And they remind you of your authentic self. This strengthens you and prevents you from losing yourself, and so the marriage itself is made stronger.

The lesson is simple. Don't abandon your friends in the rush to couplehood. And don't marry someone who expects that – in exchange for love – you will drop all your friends. For better or worse, you will always need them.

3

Why We Choose Who We Choose

In the last chapter we looked at attraction, but one question went unanswered : why do we choose this particular person to be our partner? What draws us to one person and not another? And why is it worth persisting with this one person? Why not just trade them in when things become difficult?

You Marry Your Twin

You marry your what?

This surprising and illuminating idea is gaining much favour among couple researchers around the world. The theory begins by pointing out that attraction is largely an unconscious thing. We don't know why we are drawn to this person, but we feel it nonetheless. The reason is that we are on romance autopilot, and we are drawn to hidden traits, as much as obvious ones. So people who differ on the surface *but are very similar deep down,* will be inexorably drawn into couple relationships.

Think about your own partner. You will be aware of

your differences but your similarities will, for the most part, be unconscious. You may be actively denying having the traits which your partner has, both virtues and vices. The possibility is strong, though, that these aspects are equally in your make-up too. (This has a neat circular logic to it. The theory actually predicts that you will disagree with it in your own case – though you may see it operating in other couples!)

Let's examine this 'twinness' more closely. In a couple relationship, we often have a strong investment in seeing our partner as totally different from us. Couples will joke about how different they are: 'I leave the money to her'; 'He's the one with the brains'; 'She's so emotional'; 'He's irresponsible, impulsive – I can't let him out of my sight'. Also, when things are going badly, these differences are given even more airplay: 'He's impossible!'. The truth is, nonetheless, that like attracts like. We have trouble living with our partner because we have trouble living with ourself!

How does this come about? It goes something like this. As we grow through childhood, much of our personality development is regrettably not positive, but rather the shutting down of certain faculties. For instance our clear brains, great intuition, concentration, spontaneity and warmth may have proved to be too risky and at odds with what the adults around us could handle. The child-raising process of the modern world means shutting down many of our natural talents and our qualities are literally 'given a bad name'; we are told we are a nuisance, demanding, unco-operative, bad-tempered, cautious, clingy and so on.

We emerge as adults who, in distinctive ways, have shut down aspects of our capacity to think, feel and act. For instance you probably were a better artist, singer, dancer, and comedian, at the age of four, than at twenty-four. (It's interesting that someone who is less 'shut down' than is the norm, and who is expressive and vibrant, we describe as having 'lots of personality'. We all have lots of personality but in most of us this has become hidden and repressed.

We begin searching for a partner, usually at an age when we are just at our most damaged! As we seek out the right partner for us, we are seeking, largely unconsciously, to balance ourselves, by locating someone who is still activated in the areas in which we have shut down.

Why not test this out? Think of what qualities attract you most in a partner. Outgoingness? Humour? Gentleness? Commitment to strong values, emotional honesty, physical health, energy, creativity, sensuousness? Chances are you would say that you are *not* developed in these areas, and that is why they appeal to you in another person. 'Wow,' you think, 'this person would really make me feel complete!'

When we find the person of our dreams, we tell our friends: 'She's so full of life', 'He's caring, and organized, and I feel really safe around him'. As if *the partner provides what is missing in us*. For instance, if we are a rather fragile person, and our ability to protect ourselves is squashed away down inside us, then we will be attracted to someone who seems strong and protective. So this might become a dependent situation, but it also might not, because they may help us to activate our own strength and self-protection, and so become a more whole person.

This is the beautiful secret behind all kinds of interpersonal attraction, including the heroes we admire, as well as our friends. *We are attracted to people because they have activated certain qualities, which we also possess but in an unawakened state*. If you hold someone in great admiration,

this is because you have the capacity to be like that person too, and this creates the yearning which we call admiration. If this potential wasn't also dormant in you, you would not even notice the qualities of the other person, they simply would not register. (An old Sufi joke says that when a pickpocket meets a saint, all he notices are his pockets.) If you admire a great painting, that's because down inside you is the potential to make that painting too. It might take a hundred years, but you would know when you got there.

Still dubious? Here's a real life example:

Stan and Eileen are as different as you could imagine. Now in their early fifties, he is a truck driver and union organizer and she is a nurse specializing in infant health. He appears brusque and tough, and he is. She is small, efficient and pretty, and moves and speaks with incredible gentleness. You can see it in the wedding photos: it looks like the wedding of a fairy princess to a grizzly bear!

But that was twenty-five years ago and since then they have developed as people. In raising children and exploring their relationship together, each has activated the hidden qualities of the other. Stan is now, when the need arises, soft and gentle. His handling of industrial disputes has become balanced and effective. Problems get solved, people find themselves co-operating. In addition, if his wife is away interstate he can take a phone call from a distressed parent in the early hours and people assume the nurse's husband must be a kind and gentle doctor. Eileen has also 'rounded out', and is tough and piercing when meeting with an obstructive bureaucrat or a doctor not doing his job.

When we are drawn to a quality in our loved one, we need also to realize that we can eventually activate that potential in ourselves. When we criticize a fault in our partner, we need to look at how we too have exactly the same fault, though perhaps expressed in other ways.

It's true of dislikes too

This is also the reason why we are so intolerant of certain faults in others – the intense irritations that we sometimes feel about certain behaviour. The more we repress in ourself, the more intolerant we are of others. This may be why celibate priests become so obsessed about sex, and gentle young male social workers so obsessed with domestic violence.

PRACTICAL STEP 5: TAKING BACK YOUR CRITICISMS

The amazing thing about marrying your twin is that when we dislike or want to criticize a fault in our partner, we must look at how this fault is shown up in us too. For instance, we may feel they are mean with their affection but discover that we are mean with our time, or with money.

Whenever you are critical of your partner, first decide what name you would give to their behaviour. Then see if you can find an instance when *you* show the same fault – usually in a different aspect of life. Then work on changing that in your behaviour, and see what happens in theirs. Expect the unexpected!

How couple relationships show us ourselves

As any relationship unfolds, we are soon brought into contact with parts of ourselves that we may have trouble 'owning'. Worse still, the very things which attracted us to our partner in the first place will often turn out to be a real irritation. What we once liked – they are so reliable – has become a minus: now they seem so deadly dull! Or we thought they were so exciting and spontaneous, but along with that they are totally undependable!

> Julie was unhappy in her marriage. She told us her husband Colin 'was just like another one of the kids'. He 'never participated in decisions about the kids', just told her to sort it out. 'It's no use talking to him,' she complained. We asked about their finances – were they close to paying off their mortgage? 'Oh, I've no idea,' she said. 'I leave that all up to Col.'
>
> Financially, she was 'like one of the kids' – exactly as she accused her partner of being in relation to family decisions. But Colin, it turned out, also felt burdened – by being the breadwinner and worrying about where money went. Julie and Colin were both twins in the sense they were both acting like lonely martyrs!
>
> Both Julie and Colin had to learn to get involved in the areas of life they had passed over to the other to take care of. To do this they had first to learn how to co-operate, which they found to be much more fun and a lot less lonely.

When you realize that you have married your twin, it becomes very liberating to work through couple problems and challenges – because you are discovering your hidden self. Also, there are no bad guys; nobody is the one who is the cause of the problems. No-one is to blame but you are both responsible.

In a relationship our partner holds up a mirror and shows us ourself. It can be scary to face the reflection they show us. Some people would rather run away and leave the mirror behind than face the truth about themself. But changing mirrors doesn't change your face. With a mirror you can straighten yourself out, fix yourself up, and also learn to see that you are beautiful and human.

Check your T-shirt

What if you can't find a partner, or you keep attracting the 'wrong type'? There is a key attitude to take with you in the search for the love of your life. It is written in your face, your words, your stance and your walk. It may as well be written like a T-shirt slogan across your chest. It is a statement of belief in your lovability.

Some people wear an invisible T-shirt which gives out a message almost like a puppy, or a small child. It says 'Please love me'. This T-shirt may get you a mamma or a daddy, but not a mature, equal-sharing lover.

Some people go the other way. Their T-shirt reads 'I don't need your love!'. This is, of course, true, but why say so? A fiercely guarded palace indicates a scared king or queen inside!

So what is the winning T-shirt message? It has small but clear writing, on a strong background. It says: 'I am me. I like myself. I like giving love, and I like receiving it. If you think you're good enough, apply within'.

PRACTICAL STEP 6: HOW TO FIND THE PARTNER FOR YOU

We believe there is a great partner for everyone who wants one. If you are anguished by the search for a good life companion, we suggest you first take a long look at whether you really want someone now and are available to love, in a practical, committed sense.

Being fully available to love actually makes a visible and palpable difference – there is an air of ripeness and beauty in someone who is honestly saying to themself and the world, I am interested in love. Time and again we've found that when men or women finally decide that they want a partner, they very quickly find one.

> Debbie was a thirty-year-old scientist who worked very hard, looked after others tirelessly and always put on a cheery face. Privately, though, she was lonely and dearly wanted a soulmate and to have children. At our suggestion, she began to allow this yearning to be there without pushing it aside; to really allow herself to ache for what she wanted, and at the same time to set clear criteria for the kind of man, and the kind of lifestyle, she aspired to. Very quickly she began a relationship, then ended it because the man, though loving, was not as mature as her. The second time she was more selective, and found a very suitable man with whom she is now travelling on a year-long working holiday.

The most common blockage to new love comes from not letting go of the wounds from an old relationship. It's natural not to want to be hurt again. Allowing yourself to grieve, cry, rage and perhaps write a farewell forever letter (which you might just want to burn!) helps you to let go of the hurt, and feel cleaner, smarter and ready to move on.

4

Commitment: The Freedom You Can Count On

Many people today are afraid of commitment. Couples often get into a lot of strife over this issue when starting out. This is because of a basic misconception: that commitment has to be taken all at once – like a life sentence, or jumping off a cliff in the dark. It's hardly surprising that sensible adults run a mile from this idea! The truth, of course, is that commitment grows in small stages. It's a ladder that you climb, one step at a time. Let's look at this more closely ...

Having a Clear Contract

There always have been, and always will be, many different kinds of couple-relationships. Couples may choose to be conventionally married, or be experimenting live-in lovers. They could be committed but unmarried partners, or live-apart occasional lovers, or just good friends who play nude scrabble! Or they might be moving from one to another. So there is great freedom, but also great potential for confusion.

What matters is not how it's described to others, but whether the two people themselves understand what they are doing together. The important thing is that both partners have a shared understanding about what is going on, even about basic things like money and cooking, as well as bigger things like sexual faithfulness and who's responsible for contraception. It's essential to know *what the relationship means to the other party, and if it has the same meaning for you.* This shared understanding is what we call the contract, what we expect of the other and what they expect of us.

In all human dealings, there are agreements (usually unspoken) about how people will behave. If you wave to a friend across the street, you expect that he or she will wave back. That's what the word 'relationship' means – a sense of continuity in expected behaviour. We need to know that, in certain key ways, we can count on each other.

In earlier times, such as the 1950s, marriage was like a standard contract. He worked, she cooked. She reared the kids, he fixed the screen door. It was very restricting. But today we have the opposite problem. Nobody is sure who does what. So we let society or advertisers tell us how to live. (For instance, it's okay for women to put men down, but not the reverse. Women have to work AND parent AND look beautiful. And so on.) Better to use the freedom we have today to make your own conscious, honest arrangements.

A long-term contract requires time to evolve. (We don't mean a legal contract here, unless you're rich and insecure and need a prenuptial agreement!) Contracts exist between every couple, whether or not they talk about it. If not spoken or worked out, then they will still be there, based on all kinds of hidden assumptions. What is more, most misunderstandings and problems that couples have are basically contractual in origin. The conversations that people have in marriage counselling sessions nearly always start out with 'But I thought . . .'

The good news about contracts is that they paradoxically make us freer, since we know exactly where we stand, and can take more risks to be our true self. (When couples are in an 'anything goes' situation, they often feel very unfree, as they can't count on or depend on the other person in any way. Like a car that has lost its steering wheel, the relationship could go anywhere. You could call that free but it's really just out of control.)

Developing a contract that is right for you is therefore a very positive step towards things going well between you. So is adapting the contract as your needs change, and your love deepens.

How Contracts Are Made

Contracts start being established almost from the moment we meet. We soon find out about our partner's reliability in keeping dates, we resolve issues about who pays for what, we decide how much time to spend together.

She was half an hour late. When I say I'll be there at eight o'clock, that's what I mean. In her family, time doesn't matter much. Now I know that, I am more relaxed about it.

I wanted to be just friends with Daniel for a year or so. After my marriage break-up, I didn't want to confuse my kids by bringing a man into their life if it wasn't going to work out. I told him, 'If you're in a hurry, then I'm not the one'. I was so happy when he understood, and we are going really well.

We soon move on to solving questions about going out with other people, and expected sexual behaviour. Eventually you must decide about financial support, faithfulness, affection, responsibility for children, time allocation, and so on. Couples in the past often found out what their contract was only after it had been broken, after someone had stepped across the invisible line in the expectations of the other person. In the old days there was a well-defined pattern of courtship, betrothal and wedding banns. People knew how to behave. These days we often lack even the words to express how we feel:

'Well, if you really cared about me you wouldn't . . .'
'Wouldn't what?'
'Well you know . . . I thought we were, you know, together.'
'You mean going out?'
'Don't laugh!'

It's important to realize that *there is nothing wrong with having rules and expectations of each other*. In fact it's impossible not to have them. The only wrong we can do is in not making these wishes explicit. Our responsibility to each other has two parts:

• To be honest about our needs and expectations
• To only make commitments we intend to keep

Evolving a Contract That's Right for You

Success with small areas of agreement makes us feel safer about making longer or larger commitments. There is no need to jump into deep water straightaway, and you would be rightly suspicious of someone who wanted to.

A contract is an individual and changing thing, fitting to a couple's unique needs, personalities, ages and changing circumstance. (In *The Secret of Happy Children* we mentioned the couple in their nineties who couldn't stand the sight of each other but had waited to get divorced 'until the children had died!'.)

If you are wary of contracts, no problem; just make them short term. For instance, a couple who are avoiding addressing some deep conflicts (for fear of breaking up) may contract to stay together for six months, whatever happens. Then it is safer for them to argue and sort out their problems without the threat of a walk-out taking place. At the end of six months they can decide whether to 'extend'.

Isn't Commitment a Kind of Prison?

Many people today are afraid of making a commitment. So they waste years of their life, holding back, as if this will solve the problem. At the heart of it, they fear being caught in conflict and distress which cannot be resolved. So they stay uncommitted and lonely, rather than risk being trapped. There is a wide range of options in between however.

PRACTICAL STEP 7: DECIDING WHETHER TO MARRY

There have been two radical suggestions made lately by people experienced in marriage matters. The first is the reappearance of betrothal. The second is the concept of a 'forever marriage', but only for the really tough. Intrigued? Read on.

Bishop Shelby Spong, the hard-headed, free-thinking Bishop of New York, suggests in his book *Living in Sin? A Bishop Rethinks Sexuality* that young couples need a better deal. He argues that since so many young people today move in together, we should give this more significance and honour, which he calls 'betrothal'. The idea of betrothal means that a couple announce to their families and friends that they are going to live together, have a sexual relationship and be faithful to each other, but only for as long as they both shall choose.

So this is a temporary, endable commitment. But it's a start! Couples can have a ceremony if they wish, or a party, or neither. It can be low key or a big splash. Gifts might be given. It's a happy time. For parents it's a chance to be happy about something that always gives parents mixed feelings. For the young couple, it's a proud moment, a ritual, something more memorable than just moving some furniture and sloping on in. For friends and family, it gives a chance to express support and well wishing, which can be helpful to a new couple (and an encouragement to work on things when the going is a little tough). But if either wants out, then they can stop, with or without fanfare.

Now, before you write Spong off as being rather liberal, his second idea is rather tougher. In order to have children, he then says, you should marry. And it should be for good, or at least until the kids have grown and left home. Kids are a different deal, and they need permanence. (In issuing this challenge Spong is doing what spiritual leaders are supposed to do – making us clarify our beliefs and be more up-front.) If Spong's ideas became part of how we did things, then it would make for interesting discussion between couples working out their 'contract':

> 'So you want to move in but not be betrothed? What's wrong with you?'
> 'Why won't you marry me? Planning to move on? You hussy/bastard!'
> 'It'd be great to have kids. But I don't feel I can marry you yet. So I guess we'd better wait.'

Marriage: Who Dares Wins

The problem is that with its 40 per cent failure rate (50 per cent in America) marriage actually has become a lie. The promise of 'till death us do part' doesn't actually mean that any more. No-one has quite had the guts to say 'Till either of us gets sick of it or finds someone better' but that feeling does kind of hang in the air. At today's weddings the guests are always thinking 'I wonder how long it will last?'

Around 20 per cent of engaged couples who take a pre-marriage communication course discover that they don't like each other and call off the marriage. That has to be good value for money ...

If you're unsure, don't do it. If you are sincerely hopeful, but still cautious, take smaller steps. Some couples make a commitment for three months. They find that even this motivates them to work through difficulties when without commitment it would have been easier to simply give up. Gradually they discover that storms can be weathered and conflicts can be solved, and you can trust your partner — and yourself.

Remember that many cultures in the world start with the commitment first, in the form of arranged marriages, and a lifelong love can sometimes follow. This seems anathema to us with our emphasis on choice and freedom. However very happy marriages can and do arise, so clearly commitment and intention are powerful.

We've been taught to think that pain is something to avoid. Yet pain also precedes major growth and change, and commitment can keep you there when it would be easier to run away. The commitment is not to simply endure, but to continually renew and explore to build a more joy-filled, intense and spacious relationship.

Expressions like 'devotion', 'commitment' or promises of 'in sickness and in health, for richer for poorer' although old-fashioned are often what people crave deep down. When our generation rejected traditional ideas of marriage it sought to replace a social form with a genuine experience. This is a revolutionary thing to do and requires some effort. To have security, with freedom to be oneself, is a universal wish. Fulfilment of this wish is available to anyone who seeks it and is willing to do the work.

A Couple Doesn't Exist for Itself

The effects of loving don't stop within the couple, but flow on naturally into the world around. Loving a partner is far from an inwards-looking journey. Couple energy may produce children, it also sustains them and wraps them in a profound security. Secure, vibrant couples find they have energy to spare for those around them. Their homes are welcoming places, they are generous with time, money and effort. Their couplehood seems to generate a warmth that radiates out to everyone around. As you love one person more successfully, you open up to loving the whole human race.

5

What Kind of Couple Are You?

If you think of all the couples you know, it's clear that there are many ways to run a relationship. In some couples, the woman is bossy, and the man seems a bit of a wimp. Another pair might always be arguing over silly issues, like what is the best brand of shampoo to buy! On the other hand, some couples are like gumnut babies, always agreeing, snuggled up together in cutesy-pie land. Others seem to live totally separate lives.

We are all unique, and we form unique kinds of partnerships. And these need to evolve and change – the way you started would not always be the way you'd want to continue. This chapter will teach you to diagnose what kind of couple pattern you have settled into, and if you are not happy with this, how to change it.

The People Who Live in Your Head!

A lady once came up to Steve and said: 'I think I have two different personalities!' His answer was: 'Only two? That IS a worry!' Most people have three or more different voices talking in their head – it doesn't mean they have schizophrenia. For instance, when they wheel out the dessert trolley at your favourite restaurant, just listen to your thoughts: 'I want that double fudge gateau and I want it now!'; 'Yes, but if I eat it I will put on seven hundred pounds!'; 'Let's be sensible here – a little bit won't do any harm'.

Who are these voices? Which should you listen to? Where did they come from? A simple system, devised by renowned psychiatrist Eric Berne, explains why you have so much inner conflict. Berne discovered three major personality 'departments' inside each person: the Child, the Parent, and the Adult.

The Child

This part you were born with. It's the part of your personality that has all of the wants and feelings, the impulses and the self-interest, the fun and the energy. Your Child department can be beautiful and childlike, or sometimes exasperating and childish. Your inner Child talks like this:

'Wow this is great!'
'You just bumped me for the second time – give me some space!'
'I'm sad. I love this holiday and I don't want it to end.'
'I was so scared when that car skidded across the road.'

The Child is direct, honest, and speaks from the heart. (though it can also be sneaky, or immature, or rebellious for the sake of it – just like a real child).

The Parent

The second part of your personality was acquired while you were growing up, by your brain's memory cells literally recording the big people around you:

'God, you're so stupid!'
'You are very smart to figure that out.'
'Big boys don't cry.'
'You deserve a rest.'
'Eat your vegetables.'
and so on.

These messages (some positive, some destructive) all rattle around in your brain for the rest of your life, if you let them. Like a collection of tape recordings (Mum and Dad's Greatest Hits), they form your internal Parent. Luckily you can update the collection; the trick is knowing what's in there. The Parent in your head can be kind, gentle and encouraging, or harsh, blaming and intrusive, depending on your upbringing. Usually there's a mixture of helpful and hurtful messages, since no parent was perfect.

Obviously having a mind with both Child feelings and wants, on one side, and Parent shoulds, ought-tos and don't-you-dares on the other, makes for much internal conflict. Who needs a spouse, when you can nag, hassle and argue with yourself! But help is on the way – from the Adult part of your brain.

The Adult

From the age of two, as a result of all this conflict, children begin to develop reasoning abilities – which in this system is called the Adult part of the brain. If parents talk to their kids and explain things, as well as providing some strong do's and don'ts (because reasoning is never enough, as any parent of a two-year-old knows), then the child will develop a good capable Adult department in their brain by the age of eighteen or nineteen. And they might even use it!

Once the growing person is equipped with all three 'voices', they can begin to function in an increasingly mature way. What they want comes from their 'Child', what they should do comes from their 'Parent' and what's reasonable and going to succeed comes from their Adult, and all can be weighed up. At least that's the theory! One thing's for sure: by the time you are grown up and ready to relate to other adults, you have a crowd scene in your head; a continual, wonderfully complex internal dialogue with yourself.

When your parts meet theirs!

Now, we are ready to look at couple communication. The combination of two people, each with a choice of three 'departments' from which to respond, gives a lot of possibilities. Will their Parent lecture your Child? Will your Adults have a mature discussion about finances? Or will your Child and theirs come out to play?

If you have a particular aspect of your life as a couple that is always causing problems, then this kind of analysis can be of great help. You can decide which part of your personality – Parent, Adult, or Child – is in the driving seat in these discussions, and change this to one of the other two, so that new possibilities can occur. For instance:

Diane and Sean are in their late twenties. Diane is very bossy: she is usually the one who decides what happens at weekends. Sean tends to do what she says, but often sulks and is grumpy. They often have a big fight by Sunday morning. When he sits down and analyzes it, Sean realizes he is going into the helpless part of his Child on Friday night and not saying what he needs or wants. He needs to come out of there and say 'I really want some exercise this Saturday, I don't want to visit your friends'.

Diane needs to come out of her 'Parent' and instead of telling Sean what is going to happen, discuss in an Adult way how they can both have a good weekend. They try this out. The next Saturday, she goes to her friends place for some long conversations, Sean goes to the beach with the kids. On Saturday night they get back together again very happily.

Being who you want to be

The 'mix' of Parent, Adult and Child varies greatly from person to person. Some people always stay in their Parent and live a life full of rules and restrictions. Or they are continually very giving and caring to others, but not to themself. You could say they have become 'overparental'.

Some people are Adult to the point of boringness, though certainly well organized and competent. Others are delightfully or exasperatingly full of Child energy, which is great unless they are always crashing the car, never return what they borrow, and pass on sexually transmitted diseases to those they love!

The problem comes when we are stuck in one or two parts, and are not firing on all three 'cylinders'. This imbalance affects all our relationships, but especially our couple relationship. It influences strongly who we choose for a partner. For example, you may have been attracted to your current spouse because he or she had a lovely free Child or a reassuringly nurturing Parent, and so on.

The important point in all this is that, since everyone has all three parts, we can each choose from moment to moment how we wish to interact. Once you can recognize your different 'voices', then you have a choice. You can shift gracefully from clear-thinking Adult to playful Child to caring strong Parent as the need arises.

The Four 'Cs' of Couple Communication

There are four excellent ways we can mix our three 'personalities' with our partners. These are Caring, Co-valuing, Co-operating, and Closeness. Here goes.

Caring: Parent → Child

Everyone needs to depend, and be cared for, and receive nurturance, from time to time. There is nothing quite like knowing that another person wants your happiness. New couples do this a lot, kindness of word, and touch, and thoughtfulness, are very much a part of courtship behaviour. When we fall in love, such actions are easy to offer and received appreciatively.

Of course it can easily become gooey and a bit claustrophobic: 'shall I stir your tea for you?'. 'Thank you mother!'

Sometimes under the pressure of day-to-day life, partners become less giving, or worse still, they don't notice or appreciate what is routinely given. They start to take each other for granted.

In times past, couples often followed a stereotype by which all the nurturing was done by the woman for the man (who had 'brought home the bacon', and so need do nothing else!). Okay, if that's the contract, but it is not a way to foster closeness. Better to care for one another interchangeably.

PRACTICAL STEP 8: ASK FOR WHAT YOU WANT

To increase the amount of caring, speak up about what you want. Don't try and read your partner's mind, or expect them to read yours. Ask for nurturance in straight ways, by negotiation. For instance consider spending time giving non-sexual massage, preparing a meal for the other person, listening to your partner talk over a problem which does not concern you directly. If you want some compliments, because your day has been a bit taxing, just ask! 'Please tell me what you like about me!'

Co-valuing: Parent → Parent

Talk over your values, beliefs, aspirations, child-raising ideals, whenever you get the chance. This is the dreaming and big picture department. By doing this you develop a common ground about where your lives are going, and what you see as being of value. There is no need to struggle for agreement – simply airing and exploring ideas will lead to a meshing of paths. Think of trees in a forest. Slowly over decades their roots and branches entwine, yet they always remain distinct and different. Thus individual goals can be known and reached in (more or less) complete harmony with the other person.

Couples may go for a long time without ever talking about the really big questions (such as 'what are we doing with our lives?'). Sometimes a long car trip or a holiday gives you the chance to discuss long-range ideas and thoughts. Certain experiences can trigger a big deep-and-meaningful session: when we first saw the film *The Big Chill* we sat up almost until dawn talking about where we had been and where we were going.

Compatibility of direction isn't about getting a perfect 'fit' – it's an ongoing style of communicating, a way of airing differences and changes constantly so that we know and support each other's goals.

Co-operating: Adult → Adult

Much of day-to-day life is simply a matter of practicalities. Transport arrangements, allocating money, shopping, schooling, childcare, chores and who will do what and when. Keep this discussion unemotional and objective. Pay attention to detail so that things are smoother and easier in the long run. For instance you might find that life goes better if you have actual planning meetings each day, rather than yelling stuff as you run down the hall to find your shoes.

Be trustworthy in doing what you said you would do. Make lists, detail needs, explore options, strike bargains, negotiate compromises, and so on.

You can be friendly, and kind, while dealing from your Adult, but keep the focus always on the facts. The following is NOT an Adult conversation:

'You're hopeless – your mother was just the same . . .'
'My mother? What about at our wedding? Your brother nearly pranged three cars.'

Some people carry out their day-to-day lives with a certain emotional flavour always coming through. They complicate what would otherwise be simple. For instance, some people flavour their housework with the sauce of 'harried', or 'resentful'. They add some spice of bitterness or martyrhood to the meal of day-to-day life. Often this flavour was passed down in the family – think about the way your father drove the car, or your mother attacked the housework. This is your prerogative: if you enjoy 'getting even' with the dishes, or 'taking it out' on the carpet, or 'battling with' the traffic to get the kids to school, don't let us stop you!

But in negotiating these things with each other, remember that they are simply arrangements. The emotions you indulge in only muddy the waters. Thinking clearly is something you can learn to do, and the best way to make arrangements that are fair and satisfactory. Which leaves more time for the next way of being together – closeness.

Closeness: Child → Child

By this we mean simply playing together. Some couples are a great work-team, renovating half-a-dozen houses, raising half-a-dozen kids, running a business, but never stopping to just 'be'. Closeness includes all fun and recreation together, all exchanges of affection, and of course love-making. Closeness and fun are the ways in which your energy is regenerated. That's what recreation means – it re-creates you.

It includes just being companionably around each other; doing your own thing but happy to know the other person is there.

Closeness can of course include the children. There's nothing like a hugging heap with all the family piled on the couch together, or putting on loud music to dance around or throw cushions at each other, as well as gentle times reading a story or reminiscing.

Many people who grew up in tough times did not learn to play – there wasn't the time, the opportunity, or the example. Playfulness means being willing to 'make a fool of yourself', and it's something that you can learn – having children definitely helps!

Balancing the four Cs

Caring, co-valuing, co-operating and closeness all flow smoothly together in a healthy couple situation . . .

PRACTICAL STEP 9: TOUCH AND MASSAGE

Touch is of special importance. It's astounding how easily and quickly a gentle stroking touch can change your whole state of mind for the better. The need for touch is as basic as hunger or thirst. Loving touch can calm, rejuvenate, cheer you up, and make you feel worthwhile. It's been shown that a hug or a pat on the back can improve your immune response, increase blood haemoglobin levels, lower stress, and all kinds of good things!

Affectionate touch and sexual touch are different, and it's good to be clear about which you are giving or asking for. If affectionate touching always turns into sexual touching, then the partner who is less interested in sex may start to be turned off touching altogether.

Never use touch as a means of persuasion. This too will turn your partner off touch, as they sense the double agenda. There is 'giving touch', and there is 'taking touch'. Be clear about which you are doing, and if this is what your partner wants.

Massage, which is 'giving touch' for pleasure, healing and relaxation is something every couple can benefit from. It's worth investing in a folding massage table, or putting some blankets on the floor to lie on, so that you can move comfortably around the person you are massaging. You will soon learn what feels good for your partner.

Only talk to let them know what you like. Don't discuss other things while you are being massaged. Make noises of pleasure so your partner knows what you are appreciating – purring for instance! This will also help to keep your mind present in the sensations, not wandering off, which wastes the experience. Making sounds of pleasure actually increases the pleasure you feel.

Ed and Edna wake up in the morning and snuggle together for awhile. They watch carefully as a moth flies across the ceiling. 'You'd better get it,' says Ed, 'it's on your side of the bed.' 'No,' says Edna, 'that's your job. I'm in charge of primary industry, you're in charge of defence!' Ed jumps up after the moth, but bangs himself on a heater beside the bed. The moth has disappeared. He comes back to bed, crestfallen, and Edna comforts him. Soon the sound of youngsters stirring in the next room reaches their ears. 'Well, another day!' says Ed. Edna is already getting out of bed, stretching, smoothing her whiskers and rubbing her black furry back against a chair.

Even cats have the four Cs!

PRACTICAL STEP 10: ASSESSING YOUR COUPLE STYLE

Here is a checklist which will help you to use the four Cs of couple communication. Then you can leave it lying around for your spouse to find!

Four Cs Questionnaire

How much are you connecting with your partner through:

Caring (giving to, and nurturing of, each in turn)

(you giving)	very little ☐	some ☐	plenty ☐
(you receiving)	very little ☐	some ☐	plenty ☐

Co-valuing (talking over your values, beliefs, aspirations)

very little ☐	some ☐	plenty ☐

Co-operating (discussing and making practical arrangements)

very little ☐   some ☐   plenty ☐

Closeness (playful, emotionally deep, or affectionate contact)

very little ☐   some ☐   plenty ☐

We also need to have a sense of breathing space, as a separate person. So could you also rate:

Self-reliance (to what degree you can enjoy your own separateness)

very little ☐   some ☐   plenty ☐

(to what degree you can accept your partner's separateness)

very little ☐   some ☐   plenty ☐

From completing this questionnaire, it will be very clear to you what's there for you, and what's not there, in your relationship at the moment. You may want to talk about this with your partner and find out how it is for them. Perhaps you will want to give time for the missing aspects, and this might really help you to enjoy your life together.

Letting Go of Patterns You No Longer Need

Caring, co-valuing, co-operating and closeness are all needed for a flowing sustained relationship. Too much of any one can become a problem. Sometimes people get stuck in one mode of being, and don't move beyond it. There are three classic ways this can happen. If you can spot them, you can move out of them before you get too stuck . . .

The rescuing trap: 'Where would you be without me?'

The Parent→Child nurturing dimension in a couple's life should usually be a reversible arrangement, so there is a balanced amount of give and take over time. If it becomes too one-way, then this is called a 'Rescuing' relationship. Here's an example:

> Eric had a good job in a bank. He lived alone in an immaculate but rather bare flat, drove a second-hand Audi, and stayed home at nights with his computer. He always had his income tax done on time. His friends worried about him (he was thirty-one and nearly over the hill) and they invited him out to parties when they remembered. Eric went along to keep them happy. At one such party, Eric couldn't help noticing Darlene. In fact no-one could help noticing Darlene. She laughed a lot, touched people when she spoke to them, and wore not quite enough clothes! Somehow Darlene and Eric were introduced, and talked a little, and when Eric went home that night he couldn't stop thinking about her. Darlene too found herself thinking about the quiet, tidy, shy young man, and since she did not suffer inhibitions in such matters, soon got his phone number from some mutual friends.

What happened next was one of those things that happen once or twice in a lifetime and make you wonder about the universe. Darlene dialled Eric's number, and at that very second, some distance away across the moonlit suburbs, Eric decided to call her. He lifted the phone, and before he could tap in a number, there she was. Amazing! Within weeks they were engaged, within months they married, and nobody could have been happier. At least to begin with.

If we stop to analyze the combination here, you can see that Eric provides the Adult sense and Parent responsibility. Darlene provides the Child vitality. Between the two of them, Darlene and Eric only make up one whole person! This is co-dependency on a major scale. What will happen next?

Eric has very little fun unless Darlene is around. Darlene is very insecure unless Eric organizes her life. So in a sense they rescue each other. So what will happen to Eric and Darlene if one of them starts to grow? If Eric learns to have fun, and spends their health insurance money on some new skis, or Darlene goes to college and starts to develop her serious side, and becomes a social worker? Either way, someone is going to be put out.

In this example the woman took the Child role. Equally you could have the man with a large Child component, for example, an alcoholic with a wife who forgives and covers up for him, and generally runs things from her Parent. When someone like this starts to get better, their spouse often cracks up through not having someone to rescue. It's important that both are helped to be happier and less co-dependent.

Competing: the contest where everyone loses

Some couples relate in a mirror reflection kind of way: whatever one does, the other does more.

'I've had a dreadful day . . .'	'*You've* had a bad day? You ought to try being home with three screaming kids.'
'Your friends are so boring . . .'	'Well at least they don't drop in uninvited like yours do.'
'I've got a headache . . .'	'Me too. And I think I'm getting the flu.'

Competing is based on the idea that love is in short supply, that there's not enough to go around.

Mostly this pattern is learned in childhood – from having busy parents, or too many brothers and sisters. The way out of this is to start giving more, and asking for more, in a direct way. By exchanging small 'gifts' of caring attention we discover that we don't lose when the other gains, and the net amount of love grows.

The disengaged couple: ships that pass in the night

The third style of relating is very sad, because it means the partners have given up. Disengaged couples have encountered so much pain or hurt, that they barely even talk any more:

'My husband? Oh, I think he's home somewhere. Just a second and I'll ask one of the kids.'

'My wife? Yes, I wrote her a cheque the other day. I've got the receipt here.'

One couple, Jonathan and Fran in their early fifties, told us about how they lived 'separate lives' for over twenty years, and while never being truly content, they raised their children and co-operated to keep up the appearance of a family unit.

Things suddenly fell apart though when their youngest daughter suffered a drug overdose. Their grief flared into anger, over missed opportunities and long stored misunderstandings. Communication was like a minefield. Jonathan had several affairs, something he had never done before. Fran prepared to leave and live alone. Somehow in the midst of all this, some very honest conversations took place, and the two began to experience the depth of feeling that existed between them. They suddenly, and belatedly, began to fall in love. At the time when we last saw them, they were as glowing and happy as newlyweds.

Perhaps most couples raising young children become 'disengaged' to some degree. The demands of parenting are so great that they simply forget to be partners, neglect to make time for each other, and lose the spark of why they are together in the first place. It's a little like forgetting to water the pot plants. Pretty soon, no more flowers! If this is happening to you, you know what to do.

Everyone gets stuck from time to time – in co-dependency, competing, or estrangement. The key is to notice it sooner and restore the balance. If what you have been doing isn't working, do something different. Often when things are not working in a relationship, people who are rescuing will rescue harder, people who compete will compete harder, and disengaged couples will disengage further! Family therapist Moshe Lang has a beautiful way of summing up this tendency. He quotes the man who said, 'I've been boiling this egg for hours and it's still hard!'

Using the methods in this book will make it easier for you to develop a more rounded and fulfilling relationship, so these old patterns will fall away. You won't miss them!

6

How Solving Problems Brings You Closer

He: I get so angry when she makes decisions without asking me.

We: You get what?

He: I get really furious.

We: Is that what's happening right now as you talk about it? Notice what you're feeling ...

He: My chest is tight, my heart's beating fast. Isn't that anger?

We: No.

He: Well ... yeah ... scared I suppose.

We: Ahh ... tell that to her now ...

Keep on Talking

The great psychiatrist and author Eric Berne once claimed that we only need three words to carry out our relationships: Yes, No, and Wow!

Most of us, however, like to go into a little more detail. We human beings talk for the fun of it, but also to solve problems and to ask for what we want. In those moments when we are deeply understood, we feel wonderful. When we have a disagreement with those we love, or just can't seem to communicate, it's the worst thing in the world.

'We would just go round in circles! Neither of us could understand the other's point of view.'

'We'd try discussing it, but it would end up just in a big fight.'

'Sometimes it was easier to just avoid the subject. But the problems kept coming back.'

Couples in trouble often find that they 'talk in circles', that it goes nowhere. Soon they may be avoiding the painful subjects for fear of making things worse. But this just makes them more and more distant. They may fear that the relationship is in trouble. But this is not so; having difficulties is part of what makes relationships grow. As you learn to solve problems, your confidence and enjoyment grows. It's a skill, and anyone can learn.

The Needs Collision

It's late and getting dark when Dave finally drags himself away from the office. He carries a stack of work with him to try and finish that night. In the car park he stares in horror – someone has driven into his car and dented the back bumper. The journey home is slowed by rain and traffic jams. Arriving at his house, he trips on a skateboard in the shadows, drops his papers onto the wet grass, swears as he picks them up, and fumbles with one hand for the front door key. Suzanne is inside the house, trying to get three vegetables and some not very good quality chops to all be ready at the same time. The kitchen smells of burned custard, and three children squabble noisily and tearfully around her feet. Now, the question: what kind of evening is this family about to have?

This couple is having a Needs Collision. Both have accumulated a big deficit for peace and quiet, nurturing and appreciation, rest and recreation. But this is not on the agenda! Their evening together will most likely be a struggle to decide 'who had the worst day'.

The way out of this might take some planning. Maybe they need to organize a holiday, or some babysitting once a fortnight to have a night out. Maybe Suzanne should work and Dave stay home with the kids. Maybe they should move to Samoa.

But in the short term, first aid is needed. The trick is to make little changes, so that each gives and takes a little. This builds the available energy. He helps her in the kitchen. She gives him a back rub when the meal is finished. But first, they have to talk about what they need . . .

Listen to your feelings

Feelings are an instant guide to what is needed in the here and now. There are only four basic feelings, and they each mean something different has to be done:

1. If you are angry – then you need space, or to be taken seriously.
2. If you are sad – then you need contact, caring, consideration.
3. If you are scared – then you need to slow down, talk through your fears, make some contingency plans.
4. If you are happy – then no problem! Laugh, dance and sing!

So before you act, ask. There's no point hugging an angry spouse – they'll feel more angry and crowded. And it's no use taking the kids to the park if your partner is feeling sad and lonely – they'll just feel more neglected. Ask them what they feel, and what they want. Tell them your needs too. There is always a way that you can move to a solution.

Patterns That Happen Again and Again

Couples can easily get caught in a pattern. What's more, you will notice after a while that the same pattern happens over and over again! We call this the 'unfulfilment waltz', where you go round and round and nothing happens.

PRACTICAL STEP 11: THE STEPS IN YOUR 'UNFULFILMENT WALTZ' (or 'how you don't get what you want when you want it')

Try filling this in, or just do it in your head:

1. What is the most common thing you want, at present, from your partner? Time to listen, more affection, appreciation, breathing space, strong contact and reassurance, security, talking about the kids, planning the future, making love, fun times together, sorting out about money, time away from the children, time with the children (circle one or two, or add your own).

_____

_____

2. What do you do when you feel this want (and your partner is around) instead of asking straight out? (For example, pick a fight, say how sick you are, complain about something else, sulk in angry silence, be a martyr and stay up all night polishing windows, give to them what you really want to receive from them.)

_____

_____

_____

3. When you do ask straight out, how do you ask – do you sabotage it so that the person will be unlikely to respond well? (For example, are you sarcastic, do you ask demandingly or critically, or whiningly, make the demand too big, choose the wrong time?)

_____

_____

4. How does your partner usually respond?

_____

_____

5. In what way do you counter-attack?

_____

_____

6. How does it usually end up? (For example, fight and reconciliation, fight and stand-off, just a stand-off, shrug it off but feel depressed, threats of a split up, sexual holding out at a later date, physical symptoms.)

_____

_____

7. And lastly (for a good dose of aversion therapy), from which of your parents did you learn to act in this way?

_____

_____

Usually by the time this is filled in, you will have a few clues about how you can make things different!

The 'No-Compromise' Route to Fulfilment

What should a couple do if they love each other, but have very different goals in life? What if your wants and needs are in conflict? Should you meet half way? Should one of you back down? The answer is 'Neither'. Compromise on big issues is a bad idea, because it always creates resentment. There is a more subtle and powerful way to resolve what looks to be different directions. This is 'the no compromise route to fulfilment'.

Often our wants are transitory, and caused by the immediate situation. For instance in the middle of a harsh winter, you might feel like moving to Australia, but really you just need to buy a new heater. Or those times when you feel like getting divorced, but you really just need a long weekend fishing. Because our wishes are transitory and based on the here and now situation, our goals have to be taken one step at a time.

The best thing to do, rather than argue about ultimate destinations, is to live day by day, expressing what your needs are, and actually making small steps towards them. Allowing your partner to do the same in good faith. Puzzled? Here's an example.

Ian and Jan are in their late forties. Ian wants to own a nice house with a few hectares, to actually be able to put down roots and know he will stay put. He wants to grow asparagus. His wife Jan wants to go on a world trip, to cruise the Greek Islands and drink bourbon in New Orleans. Should Ian sacrifice his desires? Or should Jan let her dreams just die?

If Jan was to give in to Ian's wishes, then years later she would still dream of the trip she could have had, and resent Ian for 'stopping her' having it. Every travel ad and poster will make her feel cheated.

Likewise if Ian goes with her on the trip, then he may count every dollar spent on the journey ($30 for a hamburger, you must be joking!) and make Jan miserable. Years later he will be scanning the real estate pages, and telling her about houses they could have afforded. What a terrible situation.

What this couple can do instead, is to take small steps in the direction of their wishes honestly and openly, maintaining communication. Jan can get brochures and prices and let Ian look at them without needing to make a commitment. Ian can look at houses, with Jan going along with an open mind. Through all this, both will be aware of how their needs and wishes actually move and change.

We won't predict the outcome, but if a couple have part of their interest and investment in each other, then things will work out. Jan may go alone or with a girlfriend for a shorter trip. Or Ian may decide to go for part of the trip, or he might stay behind. Ian may pay for the house himself, with Jan making a smaller contribution. Jan may have fun thinking about trips, but discover a growing wish to take up a course of study. They may eventually both go on a small trip and buy a small house, so that the outcome is a compromise, even though the route to it was not. Jan may be surprised to find that once she feels free to take the trip, that she actually wants a house, but Ian conversely decides he wants to go round the world, and they have to start all over again! Or they may realize they're good friends but not compatible partners, and separate. If this is right, it's right! This process is the stuff of life, and getting there is half the fun.

This approach isn't easy for people who like to have things all mapped out. But life isn't mapped out. You don't grow a tree by placing a branch there, and a leaf there, and working to a plan. You plant and water and shelter a tree, and it grows in a way that is its own. Relationships have this quality too. It takes a little trust, and a sense of adventure.

How Much Do You Want It?

With small decisions there is an easier way. It's called how much do you want it? John wants to go walking in the mountains. Helen wants to visit her parents. But they only have one car. They bid! John's wish to go is 75 per cent. He would love Helen's company. Helen only 60 per cent wants to see her parents – today. As long as she can go sometime this week. So they go walking in the mountains – this time. This method depends on total honesty though, or it becomes an auction!

Of course there are games people can play instead of being honest. Men and women often play a game around danger.

Matt and Sally lived at the beach. Matt would sometimes look out to sea, and decide to take the dinghy out, though it was windy and there were whitecaps visible from the house. He wouldn't just do it though. That would be too simple. He would tell Sally of his plans, in a slightly adolescent tone of voice. She would then, right on cue, tell him it was too rough. He would argue, she would insist, and he would end up staying indoors and sulking all afternoon. 'Bloody women (he would think), they always stop you doing things.'

Sally is a very perceptive woman. Next time he tried it on (another windy weekend), she said, 'Okay, whatever you like'. He was caught off balance. 'It is kind of rough out there . . .'

'Oh, you'll be okay . . . I'll come and watch.'

Minutes later, he is standing in chest-deep icy water, battling a small rowboat and unable to even get beyond

the shore break. He gets cold, bruised and very wet, while Sally watches from the shore.

'It's too rough,' Matt explains rather obviously as he drags the boat back across the sand. Sally just smiles sweetly.

PRACTICAL STEP 12: GETTING BACK TO HAPPY

If you are unhappy . . .

1. First take time to ask yourself this question. What do I want? For some people who are used to knowing what everyone else wants, and haven't listened to their own feelings for a long time, this can be hard. If you don't know what you want, go back and think about the grudges, hassles, disappointments, that have been on your mind; they tell you what makes you unhappy. They tell you what you don't want. Now, put them into the positive. For example:

If you are angry about others' selfishness, then what you want is sharing.
If you are lonely, then what you want is contact.
If you are rushed and busy, then what you want is help and time off.

2. Ask for what you want. Some people find this incredibly hard. It's a vulnerable feeling to admit you want/need something, and you risk getting turned away. Use simple language, a gentle pleasant tone of voice, and pick an appropriate time to ask. 'Would you be willing to . . . please?' Listen to the answer, and be willing to negotiate here – on when, what, who, how and where:

'I'd like to spend some time with my sister. Would you be willing to look after things here so I can travel down to where she lives?'

'Yes, but can it be during the school holidays? That would be better for me.'

and so on.

3. Receive what you get. Surprisingly, even this can trick some people. It's possible for instance to receive a massage and be thinking about other things without even noticing your body's delicious sensations. To eat a meal without having noticed it. Or to rush back from a night off because you feel you don't deserve it. It's even possible to hear a compliment or encouragement from someone but deny its truth to yourself. Be willing to be a gracious and open receiver.

7

Fighting Your Way to Closeness

Why Do Couples Fight?

Conflict is part of life – in fact it's essential for intimacy. You are different from each other, and this difference is what makes life interesting. After all, it would be pretty boring to be partnered with your identical twin. Without a little friction life would be no fun at all.

Usually differences crop up within seconds of meeting someone and by the time you have been together for a few years you will have a real collection. In fact, around certain issues in your life a kind of volcanic energy starts to build up. Maybe it relates to your in-laws. Or big decisions – whether to have kids, whether to move to a new job or another city. Or safety concerns about the children. Or it might be just the small stuff that annoys you, like your partner leaving their dirty socks in the bathroom.

Time passes, but the issue doesn't go away. Compromise doesn't seem possible. The pain persists.

This is usually an indicator of the need for a fight. By fighting, we do not mean hitting or hurting, or even

threatening to do so. Fighting, in a healthy couple situation, is the rapid, often noisy, expulsion of feelings and information about a difference of opinion. It's the opposite of a calm discussion because emotions are being expressed loudly and unmistakably. This is not a sign of a marriage going wrong, in fact *it can be an essential step in rebuilding closeness that has been drowned by apathy.*

Researchers have found that only about one in ten couples never fights. Good luck to them; they must be very placid people (or as repressed as hell!).

Some people are amazed to learn that it is possible to fight in a disciplined way. Not only is it possible, but it's essential – for your marriage to survive, you have to be able to fight clean and fair. For instance, this means not only never hitting or intimidating, but also never resorting to name calling or insults. (More of this later in Rules to Fight By, p. 100.)

Fighting fair means expressing your feelings directly:

'I am so angry about you agreeing to invite our friends to dinner, and then forgetting to do it.'

Rather than through attacks on the person's character:

'You fatuous, libertine, slatternly overweight excuse for a human being!'

It means not backing down, not running away, not resorting to tears or tantrums, but being clear, listening, and persisting till the problem is solved.

It means saying what you *do* want:

'If you really don't want to have them over for a meal, then for God's sake say so, and stop messing around.'

And not just getting into negativity:

'Your whole family is like you – they can't lie straight in bed! No wonder I was the only person who'd marry you!'

Fighting is a special situation and requires special care because of its intensity and its dual purpose, which is both to break down barriers that have come about inadvertently between people, and to send through a message that (because of these barriers) has not been heard.

Often the message itself is very positive. Even when the content is 'You don't understand me, you're not taking account of my needs', the reason you are saying these things is because you want there to be understanding and you think the relationship is worth fighting for.

If you didn't care, there would be no need to fight. It's

when you are involved and care that the fighting is necessary. The combination of difference plus closeness creates energy flow. Small energy flows are called discussion, stimulation, give and take; big energy flows are called fighting. The build-up of anger enables you to bring out truths which you have not been able to voice. ('I know I said your brother could live with us, but I was wrong! I don't like him, or his pet llama. I want them to leave now!')

What comes out of fighting is a new level of honesty. You get to hear the things that are hard for your partner to say. Fights can go wrong, and can certainly be destructive, so it's vital that you learn to fight safely and well. But fight you must.

Beyond the Honeymoon Phase

People handle their differences in the same way they handle the household garbage: some people take it out every day, in dinky little bags, and some just let it build up until they need a dumpster! You can either have little fights, or wait and after a few years have World War III. In our own case, for the first fifteen or so years of being together, we seemed to need big fights, and made a point of always living on a few acres, where we wouldn't alarm the neighbours.

Couples who have been together for a long time say that their marriages seem to go through a fighting stage. It seems normal to pass through a 'honeymoon phase', during which you adore everything about the other person, then you enter the 'clash phase', where you have to learn what to do about your differences. Having come through at least one clash phase makes you feel safer and more comfortable – you know you can fight and still love each other.

The Deep Barriers to Trust, and How to Overcome Them

You don't know someone, and you certainly can't really be yourself with someone, until you have come through a few big disagreements. A young couple described this to us:

> Drew and Erica had been living together for three years in a relationship that, in their words, 'just sort of happened'. Long-term plans were never really discussed, they were just going along from day to day. Gradually though, things got more tense between them, they found each other's company more and more irritating. Nothing seemed to be quite right and yet nothing big was wrong. Also Erica began to suffer from recurring headaches and backaches!
>
> One day Erica read a magazine article that said couples should fight to clear the air. She wondered out loud why she and Dave never did this. Soon after, they came for counselling. We asked them about how their parents handled disagreements.
>
> In Drew's family no-one had ever fought. It was as simple as that. In his whole childhood he could remember only two incidents that could be called blow ups: once his father left the house suddenly, slamming the door, and came back after several hours. Another time his mother got in the car and drove away without explanation. Drew found these to be horrible experiences, unsettling

and unexplained. Life in his family was like walking on eggshells.

Erica's childhood had been quite the opposite. In her family people had fought all the time. Brooding silences alternated with violent outbursts. Her parents seemed unhappy with each other but often vented this at the children instead, hitting and screaming at them and 'going off', as she termed it.

So both Drew and Erica had good reasons – at least in their experience – for not fighting. We asked them about their worst fears if a fight did happen. Drew was clear: 'My nightmare is of her walking out forever – abandonment'. Erica was equally specific: 'Mine is of being hit and hurt, and never feeling safe with Drew again'. Erica began to cry as she spoke these words.

Erica and Drew were able to agree on a contract, a clear spoken promise that covered both of their fears:

1. that neither would walk out of the house in a fight, though they may go to another room if they felt scared or upset.
2. that neither would touch or even walk towards the other while a fight was taking place.

Also, at our suggestion they agreed to make a contract to stay together for six months, whatever happened. Nobody would move out, or have another lover, during this time.

The pair spoke these contracts out loud to each other. This was the first time they had made a commitment of any kind in their friendship. Six months seemed an awfully long time.

The result at first was anti-climactic. In Erica's words, 'We felt exhausted after the session, but happy, and went home and went to bed'. The next day though, something happened. Erica suddenly snapped at Drew about something he had done wrong. Drew defended himself, and it was on! Resentments, misunderstandings, hurts and complaints poured out. Drew recalls: 'I could not believe the force and volume of my own words, like a hurricane coming out of my mouth, and I was shaking, but somehow knew where the edge was. I went to open a door, which was loose on its hinges, it got stuck, and I just pulled the whole door off its hinges. I'd been annoyed with that door for months! The whole time, part of me was watching myself, amazed, bemused, but still in control, keeping to the rules!'

Erica felt scared, but mostly angry, and stood her ground, yelling at Drew, saying a lot of honest and interesting things, and the energy seemed to peak and then just sort of petered out into gasping, and laughter, and ... well ... we'll leave them there.

PRACTICAL STEP 13: CHOOSING A COUNSELLOR

There are wonderful counsellors, and there are terrible counsellors. There are counsellors who are good for one person and bad for another. Some are very good at helping couples split up, and some are good at helping you stay together. If you value your relationship, we recommend the following criteria.

1. Pick a person with lots of life experience.
2. Find someone at least as old as yourself and preferably older.

3. This person should know how to be in, and how to sustain, their own couple relationship.

4. They should be impartial enough not to impose 'their' way of doing things, but to help you to find your own way.

5. They should be equally supportive and understanding to men and women.

6. If possible find a couple, or male and female co-workers, to counsel you as a couple.

7. The right counsellor will feel right to you but will not always make you comfortable; you will feel supported but also challenged to think.

If your partner won't go for counselling with you, it is less likely to succeed. Most often it's the man who finds the idea unappealing. Partly this is the fault of counselling agencies, which have been less male-friendly in the past. A lot of work is now being done to make counselling speak the language of men as well as women. Options to encourage your partner along include:

1. Let the reluctant one select the counsellor you go to.

2. Travel a distance from home for more anonymity.

3. Make two trial visits and then evaluate whether your partner feels welcome.

4. Assure them that it's okay to voice their reservations, and be themselves.

5. Agree to leave touchy subject areas out of the counselling until they have evaluated the counsellor and given you the go-ahead.

It's still worthwhile one person going to a counsellor, but only if the focus is on you, and not on complaining about your partner or how he or she should change. A good counsellor will keep you focused on how you want to change yourself.

As with doctors, it's okay to get a second opinion. Try someone out, and be willing to go somewhere else if you're not happy. Ask friends or your GP, if you trust his opinion, for the name of a good counsellor.

Good counselling:

1. Helps you to tell your story, what has happened to you, how you are feeling, what you are thinking and wanting.
2. Helps you to listen to your partner's story.
3. Helps you to find a mutual direction – what you both want to change.
4. Helps you to make changes, step by step, and evaluate your progress.

While making you feel at ease and safe, counsellors can also challenge you. They will insist on no violence and no verbal abuse.

Counselling may cost some money. Are you willing to spend the equivalent of a new lawnmower on your marriage? Some agencies are subsidised, occasionally some are free.

Ultimately all couples must learn how to solve conflict. You can't avoid this – with separation or divorce, especially with children involved, there will be ongoing contact, negotiation and the need to be able to state your point of view, hear their point of view, and come to a resolution with any problem. Good counsellors can act as mediators and teachers in this process.

Making it Safe to Fight

Fighting needs above all to be safe. Real and imagined fears all need to be dealt with before you can begin to fight. The issues for Drew and Erica were the two universal nightmares of all human beings: fear of abandonment and fear of violence. From childhood, we have learned to experience these as life-threatening (which for a small child they are). You may well have one or both of these fears, or perhaps some specific fears of your own. These can be talked about and dealt with through reassurance and commitment. Once these are excluded as possibilities (through mutual contracting), then fighting becomes just so much noise – the expression of feeling and the assertion that 'I matter'.

Out of fighting comes grievances and needs which can be addressed. You learn about things that you do which you did not realize. You can make changes. There is give and take.

Beware of making promises like new year resolutions. If you are promising changes, make them short term so as to make them realistic and trustworthy – a week, a month, a year. People with addictions to alcohol, drugs, violence, gambling, need to indicate what practical help they will get, not just some remorse laden fairytale promise that 'I'll be different from now on'. Contracts about drinking, gambling, or repeated violence are unlikely to succeed without professional help. Fortunately there are now many organiza-

tions which can help you. (For information contact your Citizens Advice Bureau or Yellow Pages.)

You can ask for agreements about sexual fidelity, about violence, about driving safely, about how long you will promise to stay in the partnership. Don't contract for something you can't or won't fulfil. If someone breaks a contract, then this means that they promised too much. Don't accept such a contract a second time, unless it is somehow modified to cover the reasons for failing the first time. If someone breaks a contract three times, then perhaps they are lying to you. It is not likely that a dishonest relationship will succeed.

Rules to Fight By

All fights have rules and rituals. Think of children fighting in the school playground. There is an elaborate sequence of name calling, jaw jutting and lip pouting, chest pushing and shoving, and finally (if all else fails) a very few flailed punches, and then the teachers come, and it's all over. Among adults too, fighting is rarely an out-of-control thing: even in violent and seemingly chaotic families, it follows rules.

Here are the best suggestions for fighting rules we have found so far, used by Ken and Elizabeth Mellor:

1. Stay on the goal – Remember what you are fighting for and about. Don't veer off onto other subjects (last year ..., your mother ..., all your family ...).

2. Never be abusive – Don't call names. (Whenever you use a derogatory name or description of another human being, you program them towards being what you describe. What you call them, they progressively become.) Stick to 'I feel — when you —'. You can make noise, elaborate, list and detail, but don't name-call. If our clients say 'But I can't help it, it just comes out', our response is 'That's not true. It's your mouth, and you control what comes out of it.'

3. Stay temporary in expressing your emotions – Make all your strongly felt statements in the here-and-now: 'Right now I hate you!', 'Right now I don't trust you'. Remember how children fight? They make these incredibly absolute, vehement statements, and moments later the feelings are forgotten. It's like a summer storm. Children know the secret. What you let out, soon passes.

The trick is to avoid sweeping statements and words like 'always' or 'never'. And don't run away, sulk about the place or give the silent treatment. If there's a problem, deal with it.

4. Have time-out signals – Sometimes the fight becomes too much – tiring, or scary, or overwhelming, or is just at a bad time. Have a pre-arranged signal which either person can give which calls an automatic halt. (One couple we know invented a 'stop' hat, which was always on the hall stand and either could go and put on. It sounds quaint, but it worked.) Stopping the fight has interesting results. You are left hanging, certainly, but in the time that ensues you begin to clarify what is just your own 'junk', and what real issues remain. You return to continue the fight later if need be, but things will have subtly changed. Often, if you're honest, you'll have noticed yourself losing the heat of the hate and anger (say while away at work for the day), but then struggling to revive it as you come home, as if you feel you can't let them off that easy! Feelings (unlike contracts and commitments) are fickle and inconsistent, so don't try to hold them frozen. 'I hate you/I love you' is a very normal feeling between lovers.

5. Do something enjoyable mid-fight – When you've broken off from the struggle as suggested in 4, find an activity that is normally enjoyable for you to do alone – anything from going to a movie to eating a block of chocolate to having a swim at the beach. It may be a little hard to begin since you will not be 'in the mood', but that's the whole point. Pleasurable activity crossed over with your fighting feelings will help to more rapidly tease out the parts which are over with, the parts which are your own issues and not your partner's, and the parts which you are genuinely wanting to change in them.

6. Don't compromise yourself, but do be flexible – Sometimes your feelings change, and you can give and take. At other times, you will find that you *must* hold to your views – not out of pride, but because to do otherwise would be untrue to yourself. Compromising yourself always rebounds – you feel resentful, and are likely to save up your bad feelings for an equalizer! Better to keep working on something for six months and gradually find a way forwards, than cave in and feel untrue to yourself.

At the same time, you should admit your mistakes and agree with fair points or valid criticisms made of you. It's a great chance to learn about yourself and how your actions affect others. So 'do unto others' – show the kindness and forgiveness where possible, that you would like to have shown to you.

7. Accept the present and forget the past – The past is over and cannot be changed. You may need to tell your feelings about the past, once, but then move on to fixing now:

'You did that at Dad's funeral. You tried to tell me what tie to wear, and I hated that. It was the last thing I needed.'
'But you were ... '
'I just want to tell you that wasn't what I needed!'
'Okay, I was just trying to help.'
'It'd help me more if you got the kids ready.'
'Okay.'

In these discussions, always return to the present and what can be done now. It's the only time that matters.

8. Remember that the aim of all fighting is closeness – Fighting in an intimate relationship is solely aimed at clearing the decks, removing rubbish that has cluttered the free flow of energy and communication. 'Fighting right' will lead to a sense of clarity and openness to new possibilities.

Fighting-by-the-rules is a dramatic reversal of old assumptions held by many people:

'I couldn't help myself' (I'm only responsible for my actions when I am feeling good!)
'He made me do it' (Blame him – he's in charge of my behaviour!)

'I just seemed to lose control of what was coming out of my mouth' (The demonic possession excuse!)

Fighting is a choice you make, with a goal of getting closer. The trick is to learn that you can be emotionally intense without being destructive. You can be angry, and still be master of yourself. And if you find you are 'losing it' then excuse yourself, go to another room, and calm yourself down. By taking time-out, you can still manage these feelings, and then return to the discussion and keep going. You will find that the experience of losing control, which is actually driven by fear, diminishes as you learn to handle such full-on intensity in a clear and grounded way.

You will find that things actually resolve and that you get heard, but also begin to hear new things about yourself. You will know the fight is successfully concluded when you both feel more at ease, and clarified.

What About the Children?

It's not harmful to argue in front of the children, unless the way you argue is something to be ashamed of. You can be expressive and immediate without being destructive or hurtful. But only say and do what you are proud of. If you reflect back on fights that caused you some shame, it will most likely be that destructive things were said or done at these times.

Children will always find disagreements between adults somewhat uncomfortable, but much, much better than brooding silences. Awareness of the kids' needs will prevent you from being self-indulgent with your anger, and keep you solution-focused.

How much to involve kids in disagreements is an important question, and needs delineating. We believe that in small arguments – the majority – kids need to be told 'We are working this out, don't interrupt, it's not your problem'. If a child intrudes in an argument to help, then both parents must tell them that this problem is not to do with them, and that it will be worked out in a good way. They will hopefully get to learn by watching you about how mature people naturally have conflicts, and can work them out successfully.

Serious, longer term arguments about issues like jobs, houses, sexuality, adult concerns, money worries and marriage break-ups, should be dealt with at time set aside from the children. These are things that kids are likely to misunderstand, and aren't equipped to deal with. They are not the proper concern of children, until the adult situation has been resolved.

PRACTICAL STEP 14: CRUNCH TIMES: FIRST AID IN A MARRIAGE CRISIS

Most of us come to times in our marriage when it all feels desperate and hopeless. This whole book is aimed to help minimize these times, but they may still happen, and the following are humbly offered as 'first aid'. Perhaps one of them will ease the pain, give you a handle on what is happening and give you the perspective to go on.

1. Write it down – Both of you make lists of what you are unhappy about, and also how you would like things to be different. Compare your lists. This will give you a starting point to talk.

2. Time to talk – Sometimes long car journeys are a good time to converse. You can take time away together. Don't be alarmed by what we call 'catch up fighting'. This is the fighting that you have been too busy to have. You have a 'backlog of complaints' that come flooding out when you first take a holiday. Work through these to get to the happy times beyond.

3. Taking time out – Sometimes you need a good rest and some peace before you talk to your partner. The issues and wishes become clearer, and you aren't so reactive or emotional.

4. Get an attitude – The best attitude to hold is: I want to be happy, and I want you to be happy, how can we make this happen?

5. Nurture yourself – Treat yourself well, especially when you are miserable. Nurture yourself with healthy food, get enough rest, do things you would normally find pleasant like going out for a meal, watching a video or movie, but be very particular to choose inspiring or funny ones.

6. Ask for help – Talk to an older friend, or seek out a good counsellor or mediator. (See Practical Step 13, p. 96, on how to choose a good counsellor.)

In Conclusion

There is no doubt that fighting fair takes skill, maturity and control. Few people in close relationships have not felt the terror that comes from a suddenly escalating argument. Some small disagreement suddenly taps into deeper conflicts that have grown unnoticed, and suddenly it's a firestorm. One's whole life's efforts – children, home, career, and intimate relationship – suddenly seem about to be broken in pieces.

It's precisely because of this intensity – the huge investment we make in loving another person – that we must learn to fight properly. There is no need to take chances. Make all fights transitory. Leave long-term decisions and changes to calmer times. Leave childishness behind and learn to deal and fight with the constructive passion that adult relationships deserve.

The benefits are that your family is safer because there are no hidden build-ups of tension waiting to explode. You feel released and alive, having let go of energies and resentments that have been blocking your love. There is a new clarity, and a feeling that you are separate people, standing your own ground, but still feeling warm and involved with each other. The relationship has been spring cleaned.

8

Then Along Come the Kids

She:	Then there's Angie. She's so independent for a six-year-old. She's wilful and defiant. She won't do anything without arguing every little detail. I talk to her till I'm blue in the face.
We:	Sounds like a very intelligent child!
She:	Oh, yes ... She is that.
We:	Who does she remind you of?
She:	Huh?
We:	In your whole life, who do you know like her?
She:	Huh? ... Oh! (she smiles and sighs in the same movement) Well, it's obvious isn't it?
We:	What's obvious?
She:	Me. She's just like me!

How Your Children Will Grow You Up

Your couple relationship is going along fine. Life is like a peaceful river flowing and drifting along in the warm sunshine. Encouraged by this, you decide to take the plunge and start a family. And over Niagara Falls you go.

We are rarely all 'sorted out' when our babies arrive. In fact, young children seem to winkle out your deepest hangups and bring your inner psychopath to the surface. When people have kids they seem to change overnight; all kinds of emotions and frailties beset them as they try to be loving and patient and reasonable. The reason is not surprising – we were once children too. And our childhood left many gaps and potholes. Now our children are travelling the same

J. WRIGHT

road, those potholes, long forgotten, are a problem once again.

Revisiting your childhood is like medicine: it's good for you but it doesn't always taste good. Raising children starts you on a personal development journey that is exciting and scary – it amounts to no less than a complete overhaul of your own personality. Not to put too fine a point on it, your children will grow you up.

Giving up on perfect

The first lesson kids teach is humility. Here is a story ...

Every couple expecting their first baby want things to be perfect, and we were no exception. Our work background just made matters worse. Shaaron had nursed in a number of different hospitals. Both of us had worked treating families where hospitals had done damage to the parent – baby relationship. We felt that hospitals were places for sick people, and were not the environment for such a normal and intimate event as the birth of a baby. So we set out on the most highly planned homebirth in history!

As the due date approached, we had ready two fine midwives, plus a supportive doctor on call and the contents of several small pharmacies on our living room floor. One morning Shaaron's 'waters' broke with a mighty gush, and the adventure began.

Thirty-six hours later, despite strong contractions and a healthy heartbeat from within, our infant-to-be showed no signs of wanting to come out. Our midwives both felt that we should transfer to hospital. Since it was this kind of judgement that we trusted them to make, we sadly packed our things. We felt disappointed, more than a little scared, but not defeated – it was just round two. We were surrendering to the universe, going with the flow.

The next morning, our baby son was delivered by emergency epidural Caesarean, with Steve alongside ready to take and hold him, surrounded by the machines and strangers which had now become essential. It had been tough having to 'hand over', surrendering our precious privacy and control, and there were moments of intense sadness and fear for both of us. (One altercation with an unbelievably rude nurse actually helped us to regain strength, and some phone calls to family and friends helped to clear the emotional decks as we went along.)

The biggest negative was Shaaron being laid low with a huge Caesar incision to heal, instead of being an active new mother as planned, but we got around that through having an active dad. We would still always go for a homebirth as the first option. But with a big Dad and a small Mum, you can't always have what you want.

The lesson for us – as people who make our living in the parenting field – was very clear, and very humbling. Things don't always go as planned. No-one's to blame. Happiness comes from being flexible and doing the best you can.

Recycling? Isn't that about cans?

We all carry hidden baggage. No-one comes to parenthood in a neutral frame of mind, or without some kind of hopes, fears, or expectations. Your childhood has made you expert in at least one form of parenting: your own parents' ways of doing it. Through all those formative years, you 'videotaped' your parents every move, and expression, every raised eyebrow and anguished sigh. This data is now stored in your 'memory banks', just waiting for someone to press the 'play' button. Then along come your kids.

Parents always tell us: 'I don't want to pass my hang-ups on to my kids', or put another way 'I don't want them to have the kind of childhood I did'. It's very moving to see how passionately young parents feel about doing the best job they can. And the tougher our own childhoods were, the more determined we are to make things better for the little ones we love so much.

Yet somehow it never goes as planned. Little Montgomery won't eat the mush we have lovingly prepared. Florence-Germaine pokes us in the eye. We wanted to be calm, but we lose our temper. We wanted to be loving, but we feel exhausted. We feel that our kids are rejecting our love, that they hate us. We start saying and doing things we never thought we would. Then we feel even worse!

Fortunately, children are mentally robust and can live with a few stuff-ups. As therapist and youth worker Susan Lane puts it, 'You'd have to work really hard to screw up a kid'. This doesn't mean that we shouldn't try to do our best not to. But it does mean you get second chances.

It isn't possible, even with all the therapy in the world, to get yourself sorted out first (before you get pregnant!) and then be perfect for your children. You could try, but you'd be too old! The way it works is very different: parenthood itself brings all sorts of things to the surface, and by thinking about it, talking to friends (or if you are really worried, going to a counsellor), then you can work out what is happening. A good clue is to say 'How old is my child? What was happening to me when I was that age?' and then work out what might be upsetting you. That way you can be more reasonable and less emotional. You could call it 'just in time' parenting.

Here's an example:

Once at the clinic Steve worked in during the seventies, a family came in at the suggestion of the police. The four-teen-year-old of the family had run away from home. He had 'slept rough' for about a week, hitched around a bit, then came home when he ran out of money. In the course of the discussion, it turned out that his two older brothers – now seventeen and twenty – had also run away from home at about the same age. The middle one had stayed away for six months. This family had a running-away-from-home tradition! It was like a rite of passage.

Steve's boss, an extremely intuitive family therapist, asked the father, 'Where did you run when you were fourteen?'

The father almost fell off his chair. He too had had a massive fight with his old man at the age of fourteen and left home – for good! He'd pretty much forgotten it. 'But what did that have to do with now?' The boys conferred and all agreed that when they were about fourteen, their father became impossible to live with – picky and nagging, and drove them mad. Each had decided, 'I've got to get out of here.' After they returned, dad seemed to calm down, and things worked out okay – till the next brother turned fourteen!

The concept of 'recycling' means that whatever the age your children are, you will be 'recycling' that age and stage as well – going through similar feelings, and remembering what was done with you. It's more so with the same sex child. (It also gets complicated if you have a lot of kids.)

Recycling can even happen before your children are born – conception and pregnancy are powerful triggers for past experience.

Ian and Julie were patients of ours, both professionals in their early thirties. We'll let Ian tell the story ...

For a long time in our relationship, Julie and I did not feel ready to have kids. Over a ten-year period, we became experts at fertility control! When we finally felt ready to start a family, we went ahead and Julie got pregnant straight away. So far so good. But as Julie's belly swelled up, and we began to make plans for the birth (still three or four months away), I found a frequent sense of unease coming over me, which I could not easily pin down.

The feeling didn't go away, and it was clear I was frightened. We discussed it, and at Julie's invitation I did some searching into the thoughts and images I had in my mind about birth. Sure enough, when I thought about the coming birth there were vague but recurrent images of knives, and especially of blood. Then one day, as I was working in the garden, it came to me. I remembered some facts I hadn't thought about for years.

I grew up in New Zealand in the early 1960s, the older of two children. I was nearly three when my mother must have become pregnant with my sister. I wasn't told this, my parents were old-fashioned and didn't talk about things the way we do now. Unknown to me until many years later, my mother developed a condition in mid-pregnancy which was dangerous and which required her to spend the final three months in a distant hospital. This was never explained to me – it was adult business. One morning I simply awoke to find my mother gone, and a little set of toy cowboys and Indians to play with set out on the kitchen table. A present from Mum, as my Dad explained. Even now as I write about this I feel tears come to my eyes – for myself, but also for Mum and Dad, trying to do their best – buying these toys to distract me from my mother vanishing! Who knows what fears and dreads my mother must have felt as she packed her bags and slipped away to hospital.

Hospitals were awful places then, and child visitors were never allowed. My father had to keep working, and could only travel to see my mother once a week himself, but each time he would bring back a small toy from her. He must have been going through hell too. One bright day, though, we were reunited with Mum, pale and thin but quite alive, with a glowing new baby girl, and family life began again.

Back in the present, thirty years later, as I confronted my feelings, it boiled down to the irrational fear that Julie, being pregnant, would inexplicably disappear. Also that there would be blood, and that death was a possibility. The same thoughts that must have pre-occupied my father's mind, and been whispered above my head, thirty years before. It was a relief to get this onto the surface.

Ian and Julie showed a lot of common sense and sensitivity. They used this information to make some changes. The first thing they did was *to accept Ian's feelings as real, and not discount them*. Then they actually made an agreement to deal with the fears in a practical way – *not to be separated, physically, at any stage once the birth began.* Thirdly (and you may raise your eyebrows at this), Julie affirmed to Ian *that she would not die in childbirth.* He found this profoundly moving, both of them cried and hugged each other, and the couple were able to relax and, in the event, have a good birth.

Instances of the past mingling with the present, like the two stories we have just heard, are happening in our lives all the time. If we can recognize these intense reactions, and realize that they are just 'old stuff' resurfacing to be healed, then we can use them to make significant changes which will benefit us and our children.

Whenever things go wrong in families (and especially when good information and support do not seem to be helping as they should), then we look to the recycling mechanism to see if something is going on.

So that's why I sometimes feel young

Every parent knows that children grow through stages. Newborns are in an absorbing and passive stage, where the main issues are safety and closeness. Two-year-olds are learning to deal with a world that sometimes says no. Three- to five-year-olds are into exploration. For school-aged children learning to think, socializing, and independence each in their turn become issues. By age twelve, we reach a plateau, then adolescence sends us right through the whole thing again, but with turbo-charged hormones to add to the excitement.

Parenthood brings the sequence into sharp focus yet again, so that being a parent is like having a second childhood! If the stages your child is passing through have been resolved by you already, they will not be a problem. If they are still raw or unfinished, they will be drawn to your attention continually until you resolve them for yourself, and can thus help your child too.

But I had a normal childhood

Everyone thinks their childhood was normal. It's only with the perspective of adulthood that we can see what was really going on. If you were never beaten up beyond an occasional smack, not sexually abused, not in any bus crashes or house fires, then you might think, 'My childhood was great', and we wouldn't argue with this.

But a normal childhood for the twentieth century is far from normal in the sense of being what human beings really need. The more we learn about healthy child-rearing, from the study of different times and places, the worse a twentieth century childhood begins to look.

For instance most infants growing up in the first two thirds of the twentieth century did not get anywhere near enough touching, massaging, or holding, and they certainly did not often get these basic forms of contact from relaxed and self-loving adults. Toddlerhood was often stern and restrictive. Schooling for most of the century was heavily overstructured, with a hundred rules and restrictions, and the child was forced to sit still and concentrate on dull material. Discipline at home was often based on shame or fear. In adolescence much basic information was withheld, leaving many young adults riddled with doubts and guilt about sex and relationships.

And of course the twentieth century was full of wars, depressions, waves of migration, separations, which left people emotionally damaged in their ability to parent and love. If, in spite of this, you had a good childhood – then you were lucky!

However human beings are very resilient, and many people make good lives from tough beginnings.

Key Stages in Your Life and Theirs

Let's examine some of these specific stages now. (You may want to read straight on, or jump ahead to the stage that is currently making your life interesting.)

Getting birth right

For many years in developed countries, babies born in hospital were routinely taken away from their mothers to a 'nursery' at birth, so that mother could 'rest'. Other cultures would find this horrific, but somehow, in the overmedicalized decades from the 1940s onwards, it became the norm. Some babies would cry continually, others would lie in a depressed state that was seen as being 'a good baby'.

The work of people like Penelope Leach, Sheila Kitzinger, Frederic Leboyer and Michael Odent has met with acclaim among parents because it confirms a deep intuitive sense about how birth should be. Freedom to give birth in a comfortable posture, instead of hung up in stirrups, the presence of fathers and support people, the avoidance of unnecessary procedures (such as routine cutting, chemical inductions, or unwarranted Caesareans), and of course the mother and child rooming together after the birth, are finally being reinstated.

Bonding to both parents just after birth is very easy if accompanied by skin-to-skin contact, natural smells and the chance for the infant to immediately suckle. The first thirty minutes of life can create in the newborn child a sense of safety and a trust that will be a foundation for all their loving experiences thereafter.

The disruptive hospital birth practices over approximately the last three generations have led to a recycling issue for many women entering new parenthood. Mothers who were themselves born under the old regime are now having babies of their own. One theory of post-natal depression is that it is caused by recycling of the mother's own birth separation. As she now gives birth herself, the smells, sensations and primitive memories recall her own birth scene, and a deep memory of loss and loneliness may sweep over her.

The syndrome known as post-natal depression is common and widespread in Western countries, yet in some cultures it is virtually unknown. Many mothers we have spoken with have supported this theory from their own experiences. It is an area which needs further study.

Whatever the causes of PND, we believe it is best treated by validating the feelings and needs of the new mother, and responding to these in a human way. The new mother needs to be mothered herself, massaged, comforted, fed, cared for by people she loves, not left alone (or in the care of strangers) unless she expressly wishes. She must have her baby close at all times, yet not be left totally responsible for the baby – a husband is the ideal co-carer. This is especially important after a Caesarean birth. If a new mother feels she is not yet able to manage, she must know that someone she knows and trusts is with the baby caring for it, able to bring it to her at any time. Her own mother, or a professional person, may not be the best as they might 'with the best will in the world' undermine rather than build her confidence.

'Mothering the mother', in a very physical sense, is the most effective way to heal her separation trauma, so that she can 'grow up' again rapidly herself, and be emotionally available to her child.

Men becoming fathers

On the cover of John Cleese's superb book *Families and How to Survive Them* is a cartoon of a father watching his wife with a new baby at the breast – a peaceful domestic scene. But the father's expression is rather depressed, and in his mouth is a dummy!

Fathers who were firstborns, or came from big families, or families where babies were adored and toddlers disliked, often receive a recycled shock when their wives have a baby. The mother–baby bond always impinges on a husband–wife bond to some degree, but many men overreact – as if 'that's it', their marriage is over! An understanding of the recycled feelings can be vital to avoiding melodramas here. Here's an example:

A recent TV current affairs programme featured a story about a four-year-old boy with 'severe tantrum problems'. Only fleetingly mentioned was the fact that a new baby girl had recently been born into the family. In between the shock-horror footage of the boy being wild and difficult (which he was happy to demonstrate!), there was a small scene which might have been more to the point.

Watching the new baby feeding at his mother's breast, the little boy sat rocking and distressed, repeatedly crying that he wanted a bottle. His mother's words were revealing. 'You cut that out. You're a big boy now,' she scolded.

This kind of sudden change in a child's family status can clearly lead to behaviour problems at the time, and also recycled problems when the child grows to be a father himself.

Most toddlers feel quite threatened by a new arrival. With a little allowance for this and some sharing of affection, they will grow up to actually like babies, and not see them as competition.

A father or mother who feels that the bottom has fallen our of their world when a new baby is born, may be recycling memories of disrupted care when they were young. They may need to be assured verbally and physically that they still rate highly in their partner's affections.

Kids' needs are big at the beginning, and diminish over time, while partnerships are a long-term investment. Both partners will need to maintain lovingness rituals at a time when sleep is broken, recreation reduced, and love-making hard to fit in. Be sure to carve out ways and times to reassure each other that you are still in love, and keep the fires of passion at least smouldering if not burning bright.

More than a breadwinner

Fathers who were not fathered themselves may not even know how to play with children and enjoy their company. But you can learn. Be willing to make a fool of yourself a little. Play-wrestling, horse games, tickling, and when they get a little bigger, sports and being outdoors, are reliable standbys.

The key to being with children is to find out what you can both enjoy. Especially for a burnt-out career-driven father, kids may literally give you a new lease of life, reviving your physical health as well as reordering your priorities for living. More and more men these days are declaring that fathering is one of the most enjoyable, most satisfying things they ever did! This will profoundly improve the emotional health of generations to come.

The challenge of toddler defiance

Anyone can love a baby that sits around and grins and goos. But as a baby becomes a toddler, some naughtiness is normal, and conflict is necessary for learning how to join the human race. Parents need to be able to be relaxed but firm, as children learn not to put food in the video, not to hammer the cat, or not to investigate the highway over the back fence.

If your parents handled your childhood by being vindictive, angry or mean, then you may experience fear in any conflict situation. The opposite is also true – if you-at-two walked all over mum and dad, that wouldn't have taught you much either: you will have tape recordings only of how to back down, and no recordings of how to be 'relaxed but firm'.

If you were hit as a child

More and more parents today are rejecting smacking or hitting as a form of discipline.

But if you were hit as a child, then you may find that the urge to hit comes up sometimes when you are under stress. Sometimes when this happens, we realize what we are doing, and feel terrible. One mother put it this way:

I got pulled up short. My daughter was crying after I'd smacked her, she said through her sobs 'Mummy that was a mean smack to me!' And I knew she was right.

In our book *More Secrets of Happy Children* we teach good alternative ways to get children to behave and learn to co-operate. Once you have other ways that work, then smacking just isn't needed.

You will soon learn to recognize your recycled feelings and get them on the surface:

When Sara misbehaves, I get a feeling in my stomach and head that is so uncomfortable. It's as if my own mother is watching me, over my shoulder, and saying: 'You're doing it wrong. You'll ruin that child', and that makes me feel worse – angry and inadequate at the same time. At those times I go and sit down or walk to the bedroom and hit the mattress, or have a cry. But I pat myself on the back for not reacting off the cuff. It's happening less and less now.

Another parent comments:

My father wouldn't say much when we played up as kids – he would just explode and grab the nearest one and belt into him. You never knew when he would do it, or for what reason – just for making a noise, or laughing too loudly in the bedroom. When my kids act up, all I know is I don't want to be like Dad. I get frightened that I will lash out, and my discipline seems very uneven to me. But I am learning to be a disciplinarian with a twinkle in my eye; that it isn't a big heavy deal.

Kids are just being kids, and they need me to be strong and clear.

As parents identify where their old feelings come from, and talk about these, they are well on the way to separating the past from the present.

Think about, and spend time reflecting on, your own two-year-old memories, however faint they are. Notice your body reactions when your child defies you, and do what you can to make yourself comfortable. When you are hyped up, do something vigorous. Physical activity will help to discharge the adrenaline build-up left after tackling an unreasonable child. When we had toddlers, our house was often vacuumed, and the lawns mercilessly cut, on the strength of such encounters!

Finally, we need to remember that twoness is not all about conflict. Children at the age of two are more exploratory, self-sufficient, and physically easier to care for. Make sure that you give yourself more freedom and enjoyment now that they are out of the babyhood phase, so that you and your child do more independent and outgoing kinds of activities, both separately and together. There's a big world just waiting for both of you.

This is the world, I'll show you how it works

From two to five years of age, there is a lot of teaching, repetition, helping kids to get it right. Gradually your role changes to a new one which will carry right through to the teenage years, that of the parent as a life-teacher. Just as you are feeding a little body to make it big, you are feeding

J. WRIGHT

a little mind with what it needs to be competent. Explaining, showing, getting children to help or do things.

The biggest mistake of modern parents is to think that children will bring themselves up. Stick them in front of a TV, fix them meals, and let nature take its course? Children need teaching, showing, and explaining. (This is good fun.) They also need time to play and to reflect so don't work too hard at entertaining them – don't fill all their time up with too many classes, courses or other formal activities. They – and you, too – need time to dream.

The primary school years

Watch out for the parental ambition trap! A vast industry exists to teach children what parents 'wished they could have had the chance to learn'.

We think there could be a major growth industry in lessons for parents who never had the chance as kids –

parental piano practice, parents' ballet, and athletics meetings where overweight, loud-mouthed parents could be put into shorts and T-shirts and herded into gruelling activity. Children could then be left to enjoy a natural, free flowing and creative childhood.

Parental ambitions – for their kids to be successful and important and so boost parental egos – are a real danger to the mental and physical health of children. School counsellors report that the over-directed youngster, the child or teenager who is heavily programmed to someone else's idea of a good life, at some stage usually has a study-crisis or even a health-crisis which prevents them from carrying out their parents' ambitions.

Pushy parents, especially if combined with pushy schools, can be a real hazard. The purpose of education is not to learn all that algebra you will never use. The goal right through adolescence is to have wide enough experiences, and learn from interesting kinds of people, so you can find out what you really love to do. To learn to love learning. To be able to think clearly and critically. To be able to free your creative energy, and also know how to work hard for a goal. School can teach these things, but it can equally crush them. It's a delicate thing.

The school years are all about discovering your own sense of direction. This should develop gradually in the form of choices of activities and competencies which each young person will want to follow, that will be uniquely his or her own – not yours.

We want the best for our children. The trick is to not turn this into a rushed or pressured childhood. Inner peace, fun and time to dream are important resources that will strengthen their mental health lifelong. Sometimes less is more.

Guarding their space to be happy

Then there's the media world, telling your daughters they must be thin and sexy, the boys to be cool and with it. Your kids are the targets in a massive corporate war on childhood. The corporate world is deadset on eradicating childhood, turning it into an anxious consumer-driven need-fest where children never feel happy because there's something else they have to own.

You have to protect your child's space and time to just be a child. This means excluding scary videos, computer games, soft-porn music clips, violent TV news, and so on until an age when they are better equipped to deal with them.

A parent's job is to fence out the lions and hyenas of greed, competition and artificially created anxiety, while gradually equipping your child to face them on his or her own terms.

PRACTICAL STEP 15: GOOD MANNERS ARE MORE THAN JUST WORDS

Is it fussy to insist that kids say 'please' and 'thank you', 'excuse me', or 'sorry'? No it's not – because the words are more than just words – they encourage respect between everyone, and they draw your kids' attention to other people's feelings.

You will certainly notice the difference that good manners make when your children or teenagers bring friends home. Some are very courteous. Others are positively pompous or dismissive – they expect to be waited on. One boy visited us for a couple of days recently. Steve complimented him on his shirt, he said 'Yes, I always choose clothes I like.' After being collected from the movies, he just sloped into the house without a word of thanks. Presumably adults are just there to drive you around! He came into the kitchen later and said 'Where can I get a drink?' We imagine that apart from a minor arrogance problem, this isn't a bad kid, but one who has been allowed to take adult generosity for granted.

Kids take for granted whatever level of comfort they are used to. If they live in five-star hotels, they will complain if they have a four-star hotel. We have to teach them to notice the efforts their brothers or sisters make on their behalf, what we are doing for them, and to increasingly take their share of responsibility. At our place, complaining about a meal can lead to being responsible for dinner the next day. Being self-supporting is what life is all about.

Like most families with teenagers, we have lots of teenagers phoning up our house. Most are friendly and courteous. One girl though stands out. She never says who she is, and just grunts and rings off if the person she wants isn't there. Even a kid who schmoozes (acts polite but is really phoney) is better than one who is just plain rude. Phoney politeness – or a resentful thank you or sarcastic please, can be confronted in your own kids – 'You don't sound like you are really sorry. Have you really thought it through? How would you feel if your brother had borrowed your CDs without asking?'

The main elements of good manners are:

1. Thankfulness – saying thank you for help, noticing and appreciating the hard work someone else has done.
2. Apology – I'm sorry I broke your bag.' And being willing to make up for it in some way.
3. Being thoughtful when interrupting a conversation – Saying 'Excuse me please', 'Could I speak to you now?' 'Are you free to talk to me?', 'Could I change the subject?' and when a little older, learning to wait till a pause in the conversation.

Everything with manners works best if you also show good manners to your children. You can then fairly expect them do the same.

If we insist on good manners between brothers and sisters, it can help their relationships to grow:

'You need to apologize to your brother for using his skateboard without asking.' 'Have you thanked your sister for finding the book you lost?'

Watch out for put downs, or bossiness, and always confront these. But teach your kids how to get it right at the same time. Instead of 'Gimme that it's mine!', teach them to say 'Excuse me! You took that book from my room. I'm angry that you didn't ask'. This is especially important because the smaller and weaker members of the family will start to feel that they matter, and their feelings count. It isn't the law of the jungle.

Using good manners in the family means respect is felt and shown equally to every family member. It can be hard work to begin with, but the benefits are great. Your kids will be successful with friends, teachers, employers, and their partner when they grow up. But the benefits are more immediate.

If you teach your kids simple courtesies, and expect them to use them at all times, then you will be amazed at how everyone begins to feel better and more harmonious.

Teenage sexuality (aargh!)

There is something especially beautiful about teenagers. You get to see glimpses of the kind of adult that they are on the way to being, but at the same time there is a fresh, intense clarity about them which makes you feel good about life. Idealistic, intense, emotional, physical and of course sexy! And this last quality is sometimes one which parents find hard to handle.

A friend of ours who grew up in the sixties, received very little information from her parents about puberty and

sex. She vowed that when she had kids, she would tell them everything in plenty of time. She was a little surprised how soon the chance came though, when her three-year-old asked her one day: 'Where va children come fwom?'!

Our friend swung straight into Operation Full and Honest Disclosure. With copies of *Everywoman*, *A Child is Born*, *The Joy of Sex*, and so on, she sat on the floor and gave a thorough and detailed explanation. This took a while, and she noticed the toddler glazing over a little, but continued undeterred. History was being put to rights! Finally she asked the littlie if she now had a satisfactory answer to her question. The child said no! It turned out mum had answered the wrong question. Since they lived near a school, each afternoon a stream of kids came past their front gate, and the little girl just wanted to know 'Where do the children come from?'

Tears for fears

It is scary letting teenagers make their steps out into a dangerous world. You need to be watchful, but not so restrictive that they never gain confidence. The best way to dispel fears is to voice them – talk them over honestly with your kids. Needless fears can be eliminated, leaving you to concentrate on the real ones! Parents' concerns mostly centre around safety: violence, cars, drugs, rape, unwanted pregnancy, STDs and AIDS. The things that matter are those that have irreversible consequences – being damaged in a car smash or catching HIV-AIDS are forever.

If we keep our fears to ourselves, they just smoulder. We can easily end up radiating mistrust like a lighthouse, and so drive kids' natural openness underground. You need to

talk about such things. You can show understanding (preferably without boring them with your Woodstock experiences!). You can also be a reality check, talking over their plans, their safety contingencies. If they are being unrealistic, say so – since all teenagers delude themselves, and can stand a little confronting. At other times they are brilliantly sensible. But there's no harm in checking.

(If you feel too emotional to discuss an issue with your teenager, talk to a friend first until your emotions settle down and your head clears.)

Kids tend to be unrealistically blasé – they think that nothing bad can happen to them. Adults tend to be unrealistically fearful. The truth usually lies somewhere between, so you can negotiate a middle path on things like when to be home, what kind of transport to use, which parties they can go to and which they can't.

Always emphasize the positive messages that you love them and want them to care for themselves effectively. That as they show they can be trusted, you will trust them more. Let go of them – but slowly!

PRACTICAL STEP 16: HOW TO STOP KIDS TAKING OVER

1. Have rules for phone use – An insidious source of distress is runaway phone usage, especially when your children enter their teens. Your teenager might suddenly become popular and are amazed to find themselves holding court every evening after school to a fervent circle of late night chatters. Suddenly you find yourself wrangling and wrestling to get back the phone. Or giving up and accepting that you no longer own the phone – the kids stole it.

Here's is what some parents do about it:
• Adults always pick up the phone and only pass it on to their child if it's convenient, and they haven't used up their phone time already.
• Allow the child to make only one or two calls per day.
• Allow the child to receive only one or two calls per day.
• Have a time limit – such as ten minutes or thirty minutes a night on the phone (whatever is right for you).

2. Children should pull their weight – The 'weight' will depend on how 'big' they are. Little ones help a little. Big ones are a big help. There are two kinds of help that children can give. The first is looking after their own responsibilities, such as their room, making their lunch, doing their homework. The second kind of help is helping out the household in general, such as sharing in cooking, cleaning, care of siblings – and making drinks for their parents!

3. Set bedtimes – When choosing bedtimes, err on the side of early. It helps if you limit TV and video watching – possibly to only on weekends during school terms. Bedtimes vary with their age, and they can have thirty minutes reading in bed before lights out. This simple step can give you back a precious hour or so together in the evening. Earlier bedtimes prevent grumpy rushing about in the morning.

4. Food preferences – The ideal is to eventually be able to cook the one nutritious meal and have all the family enjoy it together, so while taking into account the needs of very small children for soft bland foods and some children's allergies, gradually but determinedly keep introducing normal, adult-friendly meals.

5. What's good for them is good for you – You aren't at odds with your children. What is good for children is also good for parents, if you look at it very closely. For instance:

A baby needs rest	And so do you.
A toddler needs to get out and about	You need to let them walk on their own legs

Kids need to see their friends and go to their houses

You need to have kid-free time, and to see your friends too.

As kids get older, they need practice with independence,

So encourage them to bike, bus, walk and make arrangements themselves (with you keeping a safe overview).

They need money to get what they want (music, magazines, clothes)

So encourage them to contribute and earn money, find jobs after school and on weekends.

They need to stay safe and out of danger from crime, car accidents, drugs,

And you need to know they are safe.

They need to learn to keep commitments

And you need them to be reliable.

They need to make decisions

And you need them to be responsible for themselves, and their own outcomes.

Keep talking

We think it was Bill Cosby who once said: 'My daughter went into the bathroom at thirteen and came out again six years later'. He was joking, but it is easy for teenagers and parents to live in separate worlds. Don't let this happen – they are not ready at fourteen or even eighteen to deal with all that the world can dish out on their own. Keep talking to your teenager: be interested, polite and encouraging. Their sense of dignity, fairness and selfhood is very acute at this age, and they don't like to be patronized. Always keep the door open for communication. If bad things happen, try to deal with them in a way that lets you keep talking even if you are feeling explosive. You are the parent and supposed to be more mature. We often hear teenagers say, 'I thought my parents would explode, but they were great. I knew there were consequences I had to face, but they didn't dump all their feelings on me. I was so grateful.'

Don't compete

Be careful of recycling your adolescence in the wrong way. Mothers who wear shorter dresses than their daughters and fathers who sprain their backs while getting down and boogieing are such an embarrassment! If you've pretty much lived for your kids since they were little, then their teens are a time to get a bit of your life back, but don't try to out-wild them.

Despite the press, most teenagers are lovely – if somewhat moody – young people. Be sure to keep a positive spin and tell them what you like, what you admire about them. And make sure they do their share of the cooking and housework.

Ultimately there is only one way to help your children be happy in love and life, and that is to pursue these same goals yourself, with courage, care and optimism. If you don't make adulthood look like a drag, your kids will want to become adults. If you are honest about its difficulties, they will not want to rush into it headlong. If you strike a good balance of happiness and hard work, it's likely your kids will too.

The experience of parenthood will leave you so changed (hopefully for the better) that you won't recognize yourself. You will have transformed good intentions into reality. You will be a more honest, friendly, kind and strong person, and your kids will bring you all kinds of joy and pride. Enjoy them.

Excuse Me While I Grow Myself Up

A woman once took her young son to see Mahatma Gandhi. She asked if he would tell her son not to eat sweets, as he was getting fat. Gandhi told her to go away and come back in a week. She did this, and when she returned a week later, Gandhi told the boy 'don't eat sweets'. The boy looked suitably impressed (after all, this was the man who liberated India).

The woman did not leave straightaway; she stood mumbling, and Gandhi asked 'What is it now?' The woman said, 'I don't want to sound ungrateful, but why did we have to wait a week?'

'Oh', replied Gandhi, 'I never like to tell other people to do what I can't do myself. It took me all week to get off the sweets!'

The stages of childhood we've mentioned in this chapter are only some of the many typical challenges that families pass through. Once you realize that childhood changes also require growth in you as parents, then life is much less puzzling.

Recycling is not a mystical event. It is purely physical, triggered by certain stimuli – the signs, sounds, words and smells associated with the age your children are passing through. One way to use this fact is to simply ask yourself on 'bad' days or at difficult times, 'How old am I feeling right now?', and then organize some of what you need (and needed at that age) in order to feel good. For example, if you feel like a baby, then find at least a few minutes a day to 'baby' yourself; if you feel boxed in, organize some way to get at least a few minutes of freedom each day.

Use your kids' needs and reactions as a clue: little children fire off one set of responses, teenagers another. You will find that parenthood becomes literally a return trip through your own childhood, in slow episodes, teaching and healing you all the way.

Conscious parenting

Through the process of recycling, you will grow yourself up – hopefully just ahead of your children. Newborns will help you to learn to feel safe in the world, so that you can pass this on to them. The care of a totally vulnerable little child will show you the preciousness of life. Toddlers will teach you about independence and dealing with limits. Two-year-olds will teach you how to be assertive. School-age children will light you up to the creative and exploratory possibilities of the world. Teenagers will rekindle your sociability, your wish to be free, and recall the ups and downs of first loves and intense romances. Hopefully this will make you more sympathetic.

Grown children leaving home will remind you of endings and mortality (and also set you free for another half a lifetime!). Even if you do nothing overtly or deliberately, the awareness of this process will change what is happening to you, and your children, for the better. You will do a better job than your parents did for you, because you will build on the start you were given. There will be surprises as old memories and the feelings attached to them fire off in your brain cells and add richness to the things that happen in the here-and-now.

Much recycling is positive. If adults delighted in you as a young person, it is nostalgic delight to pass on the same permissions and praise to your own and other youngsters. The secret of parenthood, and partnering, is to be increasingly and intensely self-aware and to be attuned to your own growing edge, so that your actions are conscious and deliberately chosen, rather than being driven and reactive.

Often in our parenting job (speaking personally), we find that we react automatically – off the cuff – in ways we don't much like. We hear our own voice speaking and think: 'Oh yuk, I can't believe I said that'. That's okay! The kids and situations will just keep on recurring till you get it right. (Isn't that helpful of them!)

Give up on perfection. Be happy to be a learner. If the Buddhists are right, when you are perfect you die! Where's the fun in that? Simply do the best you can at the time. The human race is a relay race in which you do your sprint and then pass on the baton. Your parents did their best;

you'll do your part as consciously as you can; your kids will do theirs; and our whole two-legged, furry-headed species will make its way onwards!

9

The Sex–Romance Alliance

When your kids come along, they take up a lot of time and energy and the couple relationship can easily get neglected and start to suffer as a result. Yet our kids would prefer us not to get divorced. Therefore it's in their interests too that we invest some care to keeping love alive.

Australian researcher Dr Moira Eastman carried out some important research into a very useful question: what makes some families succeed and be happy? What she found out gives high priority to looking after your couple relationship:

The parents are the architects of the family system. Their relationship is the foundation stone of the whole family's wellbeing. In the happiest families, researchers found a unique bond of love between the spouses – a relationship of equals who genuinely respected each other. The marital relationship was the strongest bond in the family. Because the relationship between the spouses is intimate, close, supportive and sustaining, there is no need for either one to turn to one of the children in search of support or companionship. When you spend some time with a family like this you get the sense that the family motor is powered by two strong engines pulling together. There is also the sense that the parents are operating well within their capacity. They don't seem overstressed, or overwhelmed by their responsibilities.

Makes you feel envious doesn't it! So the big question is: how do you stay in love as a couple, while being so busy raising children? The answer has to be: become good at it. Romance is a craft, a skill. This chapter will teach you some secrets of how it is done.

The Three Secrets of the Sex–Romance Alliance

Many people experience romance early in their relationship, but the flame gradually peters out, and they settle for a kind of 'flatmate' existence. They decide it's just one of those hormone things that happen when you're young.

Just because love is elusive or subtle, that doesn't make it less real. Most of the really powerful forces in life – like gravity – are invisible. When you are in love everything around you is different – the world glistens, street lamps and mossy walls seem suddenly charming. Small things become poignant and meaningful. What if that is the true picture? What if that is the way we should move through life always? What if love washes the windows we look onto the world with, so we see things as they truly are? Why should we, through laziness or forgetfulness, let them get grimy and dull?

Writing about love in a logical way is difficult. Poetry,

music and art express it better. Here's Rumi, the 12th Century Persian poet:

> Out beyond ideas of wrong doing and right doing,
> There is a field.
> I'll meet you there.
> When the soul lies down in THAT grass
> The world is too full to talk about.
> Ideas, language, even the phrase 'each other'
> Doesn't make any sense.

Words can only lead you to the edge of love, you have to make your own connections. This is what we will try to do here.

We believe there are three principles for capturing romance, the variety of love that is appropriate between lifelong partners:

1. Romance and sex are two sides of the same coin.
2. Romance means treating your lover as a stranger.
3. Romance means noticing the beauty.

Now let's dive in and look at these more closely …

1. Romance and Sex Are Two Sides of the Same Coin

In the bad old days, romance was what women craved and men couldn't understand. Millions of marriages foundered over this startling lack of common ground. Mid-twentieth century man was often emotionally wooden and romantically-challenged. He made a terrible lover, his poor timing, lack of finesse, sense of atmosphere, rapidly turned his wife off both affection and sexuality. But it was rarely all his fault. Her lack of self-esteem, the prudery and misinformation of her upbringing, her unassertiveness, her unwillingness to stylishly demand and seduce, delay and surrender, would equally play their part in letting romance fall away.

This dual inadequacy meant that she missed out on the emotional contact and physical satisfaction that she needed, while he was left feeling boorish and unwanted, or aggressive and sexually desperate (sometimes both at the same time). No-one was to blame; it was just an unhappy confusion.

Today, our tradition of love and romance seems to come largely from Hollywood: moonlight, roses, chocolates, dancing cheek-to-cheek. All of these (along with the New Age additions – candles, massage oils and soft music!) have a value, because they invite a sense of luxuriance, making us feel special and deeply relaxed, which in turn encourages love to emerge. But beware: the externals never make up for the real thing, which can just as likely happen in a tent in the rain! A husband can spend £1,000 on a diamond necklace, but if his attention wanders to his next board meeting (or he doesn't notice the tentative smile she gives him as they sit in the restaurant, because he is looking restlessly for the waiter), then he may as well have saved his money! The most romantic gift in the world is the gift of someone's full attention.

PRACTICAL STEP 17: ROOM FOR ROMANCE

To make love more likely to grow, you have to set the scene. Cultivate a beautiful place and space to be together. Good ingredients will include:

• **Privacy** – Put a lock on your door. Curtains on windows, acoustic privacy from the rest of the house if possible. Have music in your room. No phone in the room. If at this time in your parenting a child shares your room, we suggest you let them fall asleep early, pick them up, and put them safely in another area until you have had lovemaking time together. Then gather the child up again later and bring them back into the room.

• **Atmosphere (making it special)** – Use colours, fabrics, flowers, incense, music and shaded lighting to enhance your pleasure and stimulate your senses. Get rid of clutter, don't work in the area, don't use the bed for discussing your finances or renovation plans!

• **Save energy** – When lovemaking is often the last event of the day, it can be a tug of war between sleep and stimulation! Putting kids to bed earlier, going to bed earlier yourself, prioritizing this time together over other activities, all help.

• **Go on dates with your partner** – Even if you've been married for forty years, it feels special to go out together, paying attention to how you look and organizing child minding. Each partner should organize dates: asking your partner out, arranging the babysitter, making the bookings and driving the car, so that you are treating the other person. It's an appointment – like a doctor's appointment or work meeting.

You can also make a date to stay home together!

• **Give and take** – If you are both feeling low energy and needy, decide on what you can give and receive from each other. For instance: you cook tea, I'll give you a big massage. By small 'gifts' to each other, you can rebuild the energy you have available.

How sex and romance got 'divorced'

Twentieth-century men and women had trouble in the romance department, because our culture took a small difference, and made it more extreme. Men and women are different, but not as different as the Mars and Venus books would have us believe. Sex and romance were torn apart through the world wars, the Great Depression and the industrialization of our lives. The flowers and the music were taken out of men's lives by the factories and grey office towers of the twentieth century. We lost the magic. We men were deceived into thinking we 'just wanted one thing', and women another. Women felt they were sex objects, and men felt they were worthless beasts!

The pattern of female sexuality is different from the male pattern – so different that at first glance it looks like bad design. As if a cruel God gave us different sexual appetites, just to make things hard. But this is not so. Compared with men, women may take more time to become aroused, and respond to rather different cues in arriving at this state. (And of course no two women or men are exactly alike, and no-one yet knows how much this is cultural or wired-in.)

The Victorian era portrayed men as sexually aggressive and women as disinterested – at least, if they were 'good' women. It took the seventies generation of feminists: such as Australians Bettina Arndt, Wendy McCarthy, and others, to disseminate information and permission for women to be sexual in the way they wanted. (Today men too are learning to be less ashamed – to be orgasmic, feeling sex as a whole body experience, as opposed to just ejaculating and falling asleep.)

The excitement of the chase

Nature did not intend men and women to be incompatible! It did intend there to be tension, because that meant that men would prove themselves trustworthy, safe, strong and sufficiently committed to make good partners and parents, in a species where pregnancy and babycare were lengthy and demanding. Women needed to know the man to whom they bore children was going to be a stayer.

The result of this, in the human species worldwide, is a kind of sexual dance which is part of the most successful and loving couples, involving apparent reluctance, testing, pursuit, and seduction, in a sequence which builds up both the emotional and physical intensity. In this way, romance and sex are re-united.

Timing is everything

One of our couple workshops burst into hilarity recently when someone mentioned an experience shared by almost every couple present: the 'Bathroom Groping Syndrome'. The unsuspecting husband, going into the bathroom to get his socks, finds his wife naked, stepping out of the shower. The sight of all this delicious flesh moves him to grope and grab, affectionately but without warning (and with cold hands!). She, feeling not at all sexy, shrieks and leaps away. The man may be good humoured about it ('Well, it was worth a try') or terribly discouraged and rejected. For most couples this is just a bit of a giggle, but it can also be a metaphor for how things go right or wrong in the bedroom – the whole issue of timing and making real contact.

A man needs to develop his sense of timing if he is to succeed as a lover. He has to listen and watch for subtle signals, the 'maybe' indicators that are neither a yes nor a no, but say 'convince me'! He needs to be confident in his pursuit, confident enough to overcome setbacks and delays, some of which are real and some which are just part of the game. He also needs to be respectful, and able to take a straight no for an answer and stop. The woman, too, needs to be honourable, and not use her sexual attractiveness as a power trip. It's a very delicate thing.

If a woman is confident of her attractiveness, of her right to wait for just the right conditions, then she can organize the situation that is right for her to share in full sensual release. Both partners learn that sex is a game of chaser and chaste, hide and seek, seduction and surrender. Sometimes, too, the roles are reversed. Hormones can play a part in this – as women get older, their testosterone levels rise and they may become more sexually assertive. As men get older, their oestrogen levels rise and may make them more gentle.

Lovemaking starts out by being childlike and even mischievous. Love is playful. (This is why most pornographic films are so dismal – people being serious about sex, who are not actually in love, just look silly and artificial.) Real life lovers are like little children – giggling, teasing, chasing and being free and unfettered. The pattern of tease and retreat, chase and rebuff, the surprise acquiescence cycle recurs over and over. As the play heats up, an ancient pattern is taking place which builds to an 'unbearable' energy charge. The greater the charge, the greater the lightning bolts of physiological and emotional release. The greater the chance to blast away all emotional armouring and be left heart-open to the universe and to each other.

And it gets better. However good lovemaking feels now, the more you know each other, and have experience together, the better it gets. Lovemaking is a conversation, using your bodies as the language. More than this – as your love grows deeper, it's your souls that you are moving together as well as your bodies.

PRACTICAL STEP 18: HARMONY: HOW TO CREATE IT

As people spend time together they gradually become better able to synchronize. At times the 'speedy' one slows down, or the slower one picks up speed, so that both can work in harmony. (When you are alone you can return to whatever speed is comfortable for you.)

Each day we reharmonize as we come together. You could just leave this to chance, crashing into each other until you smooth yourself into a compatible shape, or take deliberate steps to help the process:

- Spend the first ten minutes together after work relaxing and having a snack or a drink.
- Spending time alone to settle the day in our heads. The journey home can sometimes provide this. Or you might have to spend some time in the garden or workshop to be ready to 'meet' your partner and be home.
- Meditate together as a couple or family.
- Make rituals of meals and bedtimes: have a proper sit-down meal with the television turned off; say goodnight to kids or read them stories; create a sense of flow, so that you aren't just like boarders sharing a house.

You might like to try a special bonding relaxation like this:

Together you lie in a position like two spoons cupped together (lying on your left sides, one inside the other, both facing the same direction). If one of you needs the most nurturing, that person should lie on the inside, enveloped by the partner. Both people's right hands can rest over the inner person's heart.

Lying comfortably together, close your eyes, and concentrate on your breathing. Inhaling and exhaling together helps to create a harmony and synchronicity between one another. Some people like to use imagery to enhance the experience, such as visualizing a warm light flowing through your hearts and surrounding your bodies, surrounding you both with love and tenderness.

(This exercise was suggested by an article, 'Sex, Spirituality and Ayerveda' by Rana Prasad and Caroline Robertson, *Wellbeing* magazine, no. 74, p. 67.)

2. Romance Means Treating Your Lover as a Stranger

In any relationship, you spend time together and time apart. When you come together at the end of the day, or even on a date, it is important to recognize that *you are not meeting the same person whom you left that morning, or the week before.* This is critical to understand: no-one is ever the same person, from hour to hour we are always changing. Therefore the most important part of loving is to watch, listen, sense and feel the person who is actually with you at that moment, to find out who they are NOW. So the question 'How are you?' is one we are continually needing to re-ask.

Unless we do this, we are relating to a fantasy and will quickly come unstuck.

PRACTICAL STEP 19: TREATING YOUR LOVER AS A STRANGER

Think for a moment about how you approach a total stranger that you have some important dealings with. You are alert and watchful, you act with courtesy but tentatively, carefully gauging how to respond appropriately. It's amazing to realize that with strangers – like an assistant in a shop or a new client at the office – we are polite, yet with our partner or children, very often we speak and act with incredible rudeness. For instance in areas such as privacy, or in giving unasked-for advice and criticism.

As an experiment, try treating your partner (or your children) for one day, with the same courtesy you'd give the person in the corner shop. Observe what happens.

Expecting your partner to be the same person from day to day can actually create blockages and cause bad expectations to come true. One man described this as follows:

It's getting close to bedtime. I've been feeling all day that I want to have sex tonight. I find in my thoughts during the evening that I am judging Gail as either good (conforming to my hopes for a responsive, 'sexy' partner) or bad (not conforming to these hopes). My responses to her are affected by my guesses about how she feels towards me. If she is uncertain, not playing a comfortable mirror image to my wants, then I feel hostile. I respond critically to any sign of her non-conforming with

J. WRIGHT

my hopes (for instance a neutral comment like 'Gee, I'm tired') so that she, sensing an atmosphere of non-acceptance, begins to tense up and withdraw. My program of 'I want sex and I expect/fear that I won't get it' leads to the disruption of intimacy. A situation that once held many possibilities is now frozen into only one.

Partners often become so adjusted to each other that patterns can be acted out within a code no-one else would ever understand! A casual observer might be totally mystified by many couple exchanges. For instance, a whole lifetime's sexual contracts can be covertly made by discussing what TV programmes to watch!

'There's nothing much good on tonight.' (*Except you sweetheart!*)

'No, there isn't, is there!' (*Grin!*)

Or alternatively . . .

'Coming to bed?' (*Wanna . . . you know . . .?*)

'I think I'll watch the movie.' (*Not tonight Josephine.*)

'Haven't you seen it before? . . . It goes pretty late.' (*You never want to any more . . .*)

And so on.

Another set of problems arise if, by contrast, a partner wants to act 'helpful', like a kind of sexual social worker:

Sometimes she will 'act' sexy but I know it isn't for real. I go along with this, and sometimes it's fine, but other times I don't really enjoy it, I feel very patronized. I feel like I am a child instead of being a desirable man. Or I get suspicious – what is she buttering me up for?

Faking sexual interest, like faking orgasms, is pretty sad! Sexual penetration without emotional involvement is especially self-destructive.

This doesn't mean you must always wait till both of you are 100 per cent interested in sex. While being true to yourself, it's still possible to have a whole range of sexual responses: just touching your partner in a sexual way, whether tender, playful, sleepy, or quick and boisterous, can be just what the situation calls for – not the full involvement of sexual intercourse, but a generous indulgence. There are plenty of nice things to do with penises or vaginas.

(What columnist Julie Neville calls 'sexual outercourse'!) Pregnancy fears, health and energy differences, all call for some creativity, not just a cold shoulder. There's a fine balance – the guide is always – do what feels right for you.

You won't die

Most couples find they sometimes go for weeks or even months without having sex, and it's important (especially for men) to learn that you won't die without sex. At the same time, a cycle of waxing and waning sex life is different from something that is just plain dead. Best to find out which it is! When sex is in trouble, usually so is the communication flow in your wider lives. So address that.

When both partners feel accepted and good, then there will be enough sex to go around. Remember that affection, doing the housework, parenting the kids, reading bedtime stories, calling home at lunchtime, are all part of the romantic exchange and energy building. Sex finishes up in the bedroom, but it rarely starts there. If you are the one wanting lovemaking the most, it helps if you get the kids to bed, get the evening chores done, and generally make sure your partner arrives in bed with some energy left.

Where do you go to my lovely?

The word masturbation (will someone invent a nicer sounding word?) is defined in the dictionary as sexual self-stimulation. Sadly, for an awful lot of couples sex is just this – self-stimulation with the help of someone else's

J. WRIGHT

body. One symptom of this is the oft-reported tendency to fantasize a partner other than the one you are with. No-one really likes to be treated as a prop in someone else's fantasy. (Shared fantasies, of course, are a different matter.) If you find that you are having this experience of 'having sex' but not making love, then you are probably ready to re-pattern your communication into something more satisfying.

PRACTICAL STEP 20: BEING ALIVE TO TOUCH

Men and women may need help to just 'be' together. Sexual communication is about feelings and sensations as much as about actions. How much pleasure you feel depends on how you occupy your own body. Try this:

1. Right now, notice your right foot. Is it comfortable and warm? Cold, or squashed up in a too tight shoe? As you do this, you are shifting from thinking to direct feeling. You are no longer in the future, or the past, but here and now. Sexual communication needs a lot more 'feeling' than thinking.

2. Now see if you can feel the difference between 'open' and 'closed'. For instance, notice the difference between the front of your body, and the back. Which part of you – front or back – feels more 'open' – softer, warmer, more relaxed? See if you can make your face muscles and skin feel 'open', then 'closed', then 'open' again. (If this is hard, imagine you are looking at a hostile stranger, then imagine looking at a photo of a close friend.) Imagine a person you really trust holding or touching you gently. Notice how your muscles and skin start to be more open and aware.

3. Take these new skills to bed! As you lie together talking or gently touching or holding, take some time to allow yourself to become more and more open to your senses. If your partner touches your body, notice how the sensations spread all over your body, not just at the point where they touch. When you touch your partner, let your touching be the kind that invites his or her body to relax and settle – rather than demanding or grasping. (Some people touch

as if they are a vacuum cleaner sucking pleasure out of their partner's body – often called 'groping' or 'feeling up'.) Let your touch be out of kindness and generosity – listen to their breathing or watch their face to see if they are enjoying it. Ask: 'Is that nice?'; 'What would you like me to do?' When your partner touches you, 'go to meet' the touching by 'being in' that part which is touched so you fully let in the contact being offered. A world of increased joy awaits you.

Risking being real

At the start of a relationship, we are often trying very hard to 'be' the right kind of person, and act in the ways that will impress or make this person like us. Eventually it dawns on us though, that this is just too much hard work, too anxious-making. The only way to go, for real love to grow, is to be real. Listen to this conversation between a counsellor and a man in his mid-thirties:

'I get scared when I start to feel serious about a woman I'm taking out.'
'How do you deal with that?'
'Oh, I get critical of her, find fault, or act aloof.'
'That must really help!'
'What else can I do?'
'Did you ever think of being honest?'
'You mean, tell her I'm serious about her, and that I'm scared?'
'How would that be?'
'She might reject me.'
'For being yourself?'

'Uh, yeah!'

'Then you're lucky aren't you?'

'Whaat?'

'You've saved yourself months of messing around. If she doesn't like the real you, you're better off knowing that straight off. She's got no taste!'

(Laughs) 'On the other hand, she might just accept it!'

'Then you're really getting somewhere.'

So it all starts with a little self-acceptance. It's an old cliche, but it's true: you have to like yourself before people will start to like you. There's a middle place between indifference on the one extreme, and being desperate and eager to please at all costs. This is the best place to stand!

People talk all the time about their emotional 'needs'. The word 'need' is a giveaway that we are getting overdramatic. All human beings ever need is air, water, shelter, food and an occasional hug. Everything else is a 'want'. Let go of childlike delusions: 'I'd fall apart without her'; 'I'd die if he didn't love me!'. Laugh at yourself and then abandon all such melodrama.

Conducting a relationship always has two parts, like going backwards and forwards on a swing as a child. When we go backwards, we are listening to our own feelings and wants. When we come forwards, we are speaking out, and seeing how our partner responds. Asking for what you want and hearing what they want in an endless and hopefully delightful dialogue.

Each time you reconnect – at the end of a busy day apart, when you wake up in the morning – look for what is different. Are they tired looking, energetic, pre-occupied, content? There may be 'unfinished business' left over from the day that you both need to clear out before you can connect. They may be totally furious, but not with you! If you are not feeling involved or close every second of the day, then don't pretend. Leave spaces; be separate. Closeness is a cyclical thing. Often the couples who have widely different interests and directions are the most passionate when they come together.

Even the set-up of your house can help or hinder the love between you. Have chairs which face each other, not just lined up facing the TV. If you have kids, have a couch in the bedroom for private conversations and catching up. Each person should ideally have their own room to go to and set out in the way they want. The more we can be separate, the more we can be close.

Romance is something that can permeate the whole time you are together. Friendliness, encouragement, shared pleasure, even tiffs and arguments during the day all build a 'charge' between the couple which soon aches to be released. Even arguments and standoffs have a sexual component. So-called nagging wives really just want their henpecked husbands to 'make a stand'! It's sexy to have someone who disagrees with you, but still finds you fiercely attractive. Kindness and consideration, and sharing the work, mean that more energy is available for loving.

PRACTICAL STEP 21: A RITUAL FOR ARRIVING HOME

The most important times of day are often the hours when we arrive home from work and somehow end up in a scramble of kids, rushed meals and miscommunication between the adults. A ritual which is now practized by many couples is to get together immediately you both return home, and sit down with some alcohol or juice to drink, and some food with a protein component, such as cheese, salami, even fruitcake or peanuts. Spend just ten to fifteen minutes settling yourself down, allowing your breathing and heartbeats to start synchronizing, which they will as you just sit, talk and be together.

If there are children about they will need to understand that they must not intrude or monopolize. This will mean a definite decision with young children: if they intrude, they will be made to leave the room. Talk about good things rather than 'who had the worst day'. These few minutes will give you a shift of mental state, a fuel-up so that meal preparation will not be done on an empty tank and most importantly, will rejoin your couple unit, so that the evening flows smoothly. Children will benefit from the harmony between their parents, even if it means they have to wait a little. Try this just once, and you will make it a regular thing.

3. Romance Means Noticing the Beauty

What you notice is what you get

Students of family therapy are taught to notice the many things that happen when a family talks together – the subtly shifted chair as someone sits down, how one child frowns as another speaks, a breath held in sharply when a certain topic is raised and so on. Therapist Virginia Satir, who pioneered working with whole families, would tell her trainees straight-faced, that at any moment there are 1432 possible things a family might do next. 'But don't worry' she would smile. 'If it's important, they'll do it again!'

Our sensory world is very complex. Even as you read this book there are hundreds of stimuli around you (both external and internal) to which you could give your attention. We shape the reality around us by what we choose to notice. If you're hungry, you notice all the cafes; if you're missing your children, you see babies and children everywhere.

This selective attention is even more the case with the people close to us. Let's imagine that you have had a bad day. Your partner comes home, and says fifteen different things in the first half hour. Four are neutral, ten are positive, one is negative. You pick on the negative part, and start to fight! You have to go carefully because it has to look like their fault! Eventually they do fight with you, and (there!) you've proven what a rat they are. Now you can let your anger out with justification. Or if anger isn't your thing, you can get upset, and then you get comforted, and this proves they do love you after all. What a mess!

Noticing what you allow your senses to focus on, feel, and hear, is very largely determined by habit. You'll recognize this in someone who on a sunny day talks about how the farmers need rain. Many people learning relaxation classes will feel so ill at ease with the relaxation and pleasure they are learning to experience that, in the coffee breaks, they will race back to horror stories from the newspaper, or develop the conversation into cynical realms, so that they can once again feel comfortably depressed.

In the family, the rule is simple: whatever you pay attention to in your partner, or your children, will start to grow and increase. Every partner is both beautiful and ugly depending how you look at them. Every child is a genius

and a dill. It depends on you. Notice and attend to what you would like to see more of, and watch it manifest.

If you like, you can comment out loud:

'Gee, it's great to talk to you like this. We haven't done this for ages.'

It will then be much more likely that your partner will say something like:

'Thanks. It's good for me too!'

You can show your partner or children what you like by smiling, touching them, going and standing with them – being affectionate and expressive in a casual way as well as the more intensive exchanges. Low-key and casual validations of what you like will often be the most effective.

When people have an expectation of the negative, and selectively respond to this, they can make it happen.

Develop a habit of reprogramming yourself in this way. Notice the beauty in your partner, how they look, their moves, what they say and do. Be aware of how magical your children are. How well behaved they occasionally can be! Do this and it will change your family and your world.

Love in perspective

Romance is not the ultimate love or the only focus of our life's energies, but rather a foundation from which to build up and out. We are surrounded by friends, children, work and nature. It's appropriate to spread our love around.

Nonetheless romance is a major source of human joy, health and security – a skill worth pursuing.

One day each of us will be alone again, but in the years between we will seek intimacy, and finding it, will want to deepen it. If we are successful even for a short time, then we will generate an energy that spreads out into the world around us. Life will be enhanced. Living with romance has a unique glory, and we wish you well if you choose to take the chance.

PRACTICAL STEP 22: HEALING FROM SEXUAL ABUSE

Sadly, some women and men have experienced sexual violation either in childhood or as adults. Not surprisingly, sexual activity, even with a trusted and loving partner, will often bring to the surface feelings of distress or fear. We have found that the best way to resolve this is for the person who has this history to negotiate that, if the need arises, they can take total control of what happens sexually, with the other person's support and understanding.

In essence, they can at any time during lovemaking, simply say 'STOP', and the other person will stop moving and lie calmly waiting. The person who is experiencing distress or fear should keep their eyes open and may hold their partner or ask to be held, or just lie still, or talk, allowing the fear to dissipate.

By taking back what was missing in the abuse situation – control – and by not running away but experiencing directly that this person is safe and can be trusted, it becomes possible for sexual desire to return. Through care and time, and a willingness to be a little vulnerable, wounded sexuality can be made whole again in a loving relationship.

PRACTICAL STEP 23:
CHARGING UP

The concept of sexual tension, while useful, can also be misleading because it suggests being 'uptight'. A more useful term is that used by bioenergetic therapists – the idea of physical 'charge' accumulated in the body, rather like static electricity. A tensed up person can hold very little charge in their body. They easily get tired. They will need strong sexual stimulation to feel excitation, will soon reach a pressure for release once this excitation is gained, and will rapidly de-excite once orgasm is reached. A relaxed, open body will be more receptive to subtle and diverse stimulation, will charge up in slow surges, and will be able to maintain a plateau of pleasure for long periods. Discharge will be more powerful, longer in duration, and more total in its extent through their body.

Bioenergetic therapist Julie Henderson, in her book *The Lover Within*, suggests a basic and simple exercise for people wanting to expand their capacity for charge and therefore for pleasure. She suggests that people practise sexually stimulating themselves, in private, or with the help of a partner, until they are almost at the point of orgasm. They should then stop just before orgasm is reached, taking time to deliberately relax their body. They may then spend an hour moving about, resting, doing other things, before progressing to sexual release if they wish, either alone or with a partner.

Try it. The key is in the relaxation, in deliberately making room for the higher degree of excitation. You will progressively find that you can hold more and more charge and become more energized, not just sexually but in other spheres of life too. This physical skill learned from the exercise can be carried on into actual intercourse to help you completely let go of striving or effort for release and simply focus on the sensations that are already happening, rather than pushing for more. To begin with, wait until that magical moment when you know orgasm is starting to happen. At this point, relax your body totally, especially your thighs, buttocks and leg muscles. Most men report that when doing this, they experience a much greater release flowing through their whole body.

After a time, begin to activate this relaxing, or self-abandonment, earlier in the lovemaking cycle. Don't go on a program – just experiment when you think of it. It's important to be able to receive – lovemaking is something you feel, as much as something you do.

You may find that at the height of lovemaking, if you relax and draw back a little from the urge to push, then lust merges into just pleasure in being inside one another, that cycles of pushing and just-experiencing alternate. Men who are concerned about the duration of intercourse, about 'going the distance', find that this is no longer an issue. Rather than trying to control oneself, the opposite action, relaxation, is what works. Relaxation can be still vigorous and energetic, but it is always loose and flowing.

PRACTICAL STEP 24:
EMOTIONAL HEALING

Some people have told us of surprising reactions in the moments during and just after orgasm: being wrenched with sobs and tears, or swept with anger or violent feelings or images. These are simply the baggage that has been carried over from coping with life's difficulties, releasing in the safety and relaxation your body now feels. Accept and allow these to move through you and they will give way in turn to melting tenderness.

Tenderness and adoration towards a partner are not an illusion, or a spurious after-effect of lovemaking but simply the true feelings which emerge when you abandon, even fleetingly, your normal defences.

Especially if your partner is normally the passive one, experiment with swapping back and forth the control of movement, so that each has the opportunity to concentrate simply on receiving. Allow more time and space for massage in sexual play, and for its own sake. Massage teaches your body to know what relaxation is. This kind of communication begins to move beyond what words can ever say. At the height of sexual pleasure, open your eyes, look tenderly at your lover's face and eyes, and really see each other.

Eventually you will understand why Tantric yoga treats sex as a meditation, a way to union with God.

10

Advanced Lessons

You are here on this planet to learn to love.
And that's all.

She:	(thinks) Will I start writing the world's greatest novel, or will I change the baby's nappy?
He:	What's that awful smell?
She:	It was a dark and stormy night ...
He:	Huh?

Why?

Why get out of bed in the morning? Why take a holiday? Why spend twenty years raising children?

Sometimes we do the right thing without knowing why. Often in life you only work out the reasons for things long after you have done them. Getting married and having kids is a perfect example of this. If you ever lose the plot, or lose motivation (and who doesn't) then the best thing to do is mentally zoom way up in the sky, and look down at 'the big picture' of your life.

The answer to human motivation is very simple. We do what we do because it makes us feel good. Outward acts are always done for internal goals. From going clubbing, to working with sick people, it's no different – we pursue a feeling of rightness and flowing connectedness to life.

The paradox of doing what makes us feel good is that, strangely, it does not necessarily lead to greediness or exploitation or cruelty to others. These are only the fate of those people who are exceptionally unskilled in their selfishness. That's why these destructive attributes, though they have always been present in the world, never really predominate. What makes us feel good, ultimately, is doing what is good for everyone.

Enlightened selfishness

A friend of ours, Ross, came into a large sum of money – royalties for some writing work he had done years before. This was around Christmas 1985. He was sitting watching TV with his six-week-old baby son on his knee, when the first footage of the Ethiopian famine came onto the screen. He thought about it for a couple of hours, and then wrote a cheque for the full sum he had received and posted it to a development agency he knew would use it well. He told us later that every time Ethiopia was mentioned in the news after that, he felt good. Significantly for him, the film clip had shown parents, holding their babies just like he was holding his, and he had simply felt the connection. What it would be like to be a parent who could not feed their own child.

When you were a youngster, you were probably told that selfishness was bad. Perhaps though, all we need really do is make our selfishness more effective. Ross watched the TV news with the informed heart of a parent, and his 'selfish' gratification came from helping as best he could the hungry people who stood before him on the screen. Our needs go beyond ourselves, they seem to move ever upwards. We are programmed towards behaviour which is more and more integrated, more and more 'right'.

Have you ever watched young kittens playing endlessly, chasing, rolling, exploring their world? A kitten's internal program is to, through play, become a superbly co-ordinated hunter.

Humans have a program to learn too. We never cease our exploration. Even when fed, housed, loved and valued, we still pursue self-realization, union with life, something more. Human actions in the world only make sense when we realize this push for personal transcendence. To have one's beliefs, knowledge, emotions and actions all finally moving together in synergy. Occasionally, fleetingly, you reach such a state, and it feels wonderful.

We are intended to be truth-seekers, life-bringers, but this image of ourselves has all but been lost in modern life. It's hardly the view of man you are presented with daily in the media. Every night the TV 'news' presents us, in vivid detail, the tiny proportion of places where the human race is going wrong. Imagine if the TV news were governed by a sense of proportion:

Here is the news. Six billion people today got fed, co-operated with each other, and were really nice to their children. A few slipped up, but nothing worth mentioning. And now here's the weather ...

Finding the beauty inside

The American psychologist Robert Carkhuff said 'We are born with only the potential to be human'. It's not guaranteed. Love has to be there or we do not reach our potential. People raised with love become strong, individual, warm, idealistic and yet practical. They make a difference in the world.

We all want to feel right, and so we strive to do right. All of our passions, even our guilt and confusion, stem from this. The world outside us has meaning only as the setting for our individual and collective salvation. The soul's journey is what matters; everything else is just stage props.

> A man we know built his family a house out of beautiful native timbers. One night it burned to the ground, and he lost all his possessions. They had to spend a long cold winter in a caravan. We were distraught on his behalf. He wasn't worried at all. He'd enjoyed building it, and was getting a little bored anyway now it was finished. He had some great ideas for the next one!

Every action we take in the world is simply aimed at producing internal balance. If we see a beautiful work of art, or hear glorious music, we feel its beauty reflected in us and our spirit soars. The beauty however is in us. *A painting does not have beauty, hanging alone in a gallery, unless we are there to see it, and have the beauty inside us to respond with.* The material world, including the people around us, are the tools with which we refine our soul. We want to feel beautiful inside, so we seek it outside. We want to feel peaceful, so we seek to build a peaceful world.

As you realize that *all you are ever working on is yourself*, then you develop a certain lightness about life's ups and downs.

This lightheartedness does not prevent you from feeling occasional sadness, anger, or fear, but at the same time means these feelings pass and are gone.

What you discover is that value comes from *the meaning you choose to give to things*. You let things matter – like your children, your work, something you get passionate about in the larger world. And by doing this, you live more intensely.

Raising a family is the perfect pathway for learning to love. As we love and play and draw giggles of delight from our own children, we heal our own residual unlovedness, and rediscover our own delight. Helping our teenagers to stand on their own, and find their strengths and passions, we rediscover our own idealism and purpose. And continually, our partner in this process holds up a mirror to us, challenging us to remove layer after layer of falseness, to one day stand without defences, real and present.

All the time, we are making meaning, we are making life, we are making love. As we do this, a sense of greater certainty begins to emerge, a sense not only of fulfilment, but of being part of a heroic journey with all of humankind.

One Last Story

Everything depends on us keeping a sense of perspective.

We live in a universe which, as far as we can tell, is a place mostly of fire and dust and vast empty space. On a few moist, green specks amidst a desert of stars, it has brought forth life. The life itself swirls and recombines in exquisite complexity and richness. There is more variety in the tip of your finger, or the petal of a flower, than in the next million light years of emptiness.

Sometimes we stumble so blindly along, we never notice how precious or unique life really is, until it is gone. The bereavement columns of newspapers are full of pathetic regret – things that would have been better expressed in the midst of life. People take the miraculous for granted, until it suddenly ends.

This final story is our own. Unexpected events resulted in a fusion of commitment and emotion more intense than we had known was possible. Many parents reading this will have gone through something similar and will know what we mean . . .

It's about four o'clock on a wintry Sunday afternoon. Some relatives are visiting and our nine-week-old baby son is having a nap in the bedroom. He's been asleep for perhaps half-an-hour, perhaps three-quarters (you don't take much notice of these things until later, looking back). Shaaron goes to the bedroom to check if he is okay. I hear her scream my name out loud. Suddenly everything goes into slow motion.

Already I don't want to know. I don't want to go in there, but I do. Shaaron is pulling and kneading at baby

Rohan, his face is blue and still, the pupils of his little eyes rolled back alarmingly. We start yelling at him 'Breathe Rohan! Breathe!' Shaaron starts mouth-to-mouth, and I think, 'Well, she's a nurse. She'll fix things', but I'm far from sure. I run to the phone in the next room, and start dialling the emergency number for Australia, 000. My hand (and in fact my whole body) is shaking so much that it takes me three tries to get it right. I force myself to steady down, and finally I get through. The operator is efficient, she takes me seriously, and the ambulance people answer in seconds. They are clear, calm and fast. They are on their way.

Shaaron says 'He's got a heartbeat. I think it's still beating.' I can't bear to look her in the eye. We take turns to blow air into Rohan, covering his tiny face and nose easily with our mouths. He feels cold. I remember to blow gently, not to injure his little lungs. We watch desperately for some sign of recovery, but there's nothing there. The eyes are still rolled back and his little body is soggy and loose. I feel it's not really him. We are yelling all the time 'We want you! We love you! Stay alive Rohan!' This does not seem crazy, either then, or now looking back.

Shaaron's sister runs in with an icy cold washcloth, we put it on his body to shock him awake. He stirs a little, perhaps. It's hard to tell. We keep on breathing into him. He is not dead, neither is he fully alive, and it becomes a kind of holding operation, waiting for the ambulance. Then it arrives. Oxygen helps, some of the blueness goes away. I'm a little embarrassed with strangers in my house, then forget it. A second ambulance team comes, they are (we guess and confirm later) the 'dead baby team'. They exchange a few words, then leave. We carry Rohan amidst oxygen hoses and battery packs into the normal, green rainy street. Are our neighbours watching? How could they not, our front lawn looks like a movie set. We travel in the ambulance slowly along familiar roads that will never be quite the same. Everything important to me is inside that van. Nothing outside matters, it is a dream.

It's not over yet. At the hospital I notice the ambulancemen tense up, they seem already angry with the nurses in casualty before they start to talk. I've heard about this problem. A nurse asks what has happened and they won't tell her. 'Get the resident. We don't want to go through this all three times over.' Something like that. For some reason I am getting angry too, on top of all the fear. We have a live baby, pink and breathing now, but still very dazed and unnaturally sleepy. But why has all this happened? We are put in a booth with a curtain. People with injuries and nurses are walking about, people come in and go out and a young man, a resident, comes in. 'What happened?' We tell him, but he says nothing, he goes away! After what seems like forever, he comes back. 'The child seems to be all right now. You should be right to go home now.' Doesn't he know how such imprecision hurts? We don't want to go home, we want to know what has happened and why? Is our baby okay? What if it happens again? We insist on staying in the hospital.

Casual, chatting people in the reception office keep me waiting. It's just another day for them. There are ten long minutes of filling in forms, with us still in our house slippers and old tracksuits, clutching our baby in an ambulance blanket. I am dazed and feel angry and passed around.

I'm battered by violent and wild impulses. I go back through Casualty, see the young resident at a desk. He ignores me so I interrupt him from the paperwork. I feel so idiotic beseeching this man, apologizing for intruding, I know you have forms to fill in, but what is wrong with my child? Is he damaged? He looks at me distractedly. No, it should be fine. His flippant vagueness sets my head hammering. Of course, it's a dumb question. He couldn't know. No-one could know yet.

We go up to the Sick Babies ward; they need to know all over again what happened. We recount the story, they are kind and find us a room we can sleep in with our baby.

We ask for a breathing monitor in case we fall asleep and it happens again. This prompts some discussion — if we are worried perhaps they should be too. They decide we'd better be on the ward, so we are moved back out of our room into a ward full of other damaged little ones, and other hovering parents. At least this gives us some perspective on our problems. We take turns all night to stay awake. I watch the stars through the window and listen to that most beautiful sound in the world — our baby softly breathing.

In the morning, walking down the corridor I meet a senior nurse I know. I tell her briefly what has happened and she gives me a sympathetic look. Suddenly I am in tears and she is hugging me. I feel real for the first time in twelve hours. Back on the ward, time drags. We give up waiting for a diagnosis. We discharge ourselves, and go home.

We get back to our beautiful cottage, and clean fresh air. We go inside and find ourselves suddenly crying floods of relief that it is over. We put on loud rock music and dance in celebration. Rohan is sleepy for a day or two, but soon plays again, and laughs again, and it all might never have happened. For weeks we will not leave his side, and for months we always sleep beside him, waking and listening at night-time to check his breathing. In time, though, this need relaxes.*

We do not talk to friends or family about the event, not wanting to wrap anxiety around our child.

The experience makes the transition in our minds from trauma, to recovery, to being grateful that it happened. (Does this sound strange to you? We have counselled dying cancer patients who had made the remarkable admission that they were grateful for cancer for it showed them how to live.) We refer to the event as Rohan's 'second birth' – an experience which made us a family. Our gratitude is for a lightning-bolt moment of totally unified effort back there in his bedroom – that we love each other, and this child, and want him to live so fiercely. That feeling has never left us.

---

* Some readers of this book will have lost babies through cot-death (also called Sudden Infant Death Syndrome). It is important to know that in the case above the baby still had a heartbeat, and was warm, and so resuscitation was possible. The cause of the episode is still unknown, although the baby did have a triple antigen injection two days earlier, and an unusual reaction to this was suggested by our GP.

Fully Living

Love brings you alive. One father told us:

> Only when I had actually held a child of my own creating in my arms did I really know what life was. Up until then, I'd been a robot. My kids brought me to life.

No mountain climb can match the fatigue of the first twelve months of parenthood, and no accolade can match the pleasure of your own child running towards you with arms open wide. Having a family meets so many primary needs. We all need daily physical touching, with familiarity and depth behind it. We need constant interaction to talk out our lives as we live them, with people who know and are invested in our words. We thrive on the energy and release of good sex, which only comes with trust and practice together. We need the security, and the freedom, which reliable relationships bring. We need the challenge of long-term commitments, of a story that is long and deep and difficult at times, but overwhelmingly worth it.

Whether you are actually a partner or a parent, or neither, is insignificant. You find equivalents. If we choose to, we can make love in every interaction with every living thing we meet. We are all parents, and we are all children, and we are all lovers. May as well do it with style.

Appendix

An Important Feminist Message: Don't Try to find Yourself in Your Lover's Eyes!

'It starts when you sink into his arms, and it ends with your arms in his sink.' So went the old feminist warning to lovestruck young girls. And it's just as true today – probably for both genders. The problem is finding our identity in love: if we measure ourselves by how much someone loves us, we give away our most valuable possession – self-worth.

This is the theme of a beautiful and unusual book, *The Orchard* by Drusilla Modjeska. Modjeska tells some stories of love and life through the eyes of a wise and worldly woman called Ettie. It's like sitting at the kitchen table of a tough but kind adviser and knowing you are being saved from years of trouble if you just listen really carefully.

Here are some favourite parts:

... we should as girls have been taught to stand alone, we should have been taught the dangers of pinning happiness on the vagaries of love. But while we live in a culture in which our deepest desires are formed in the family, while our hopes for intimacy and personal satisfaction are hooked to the romantic dyad, a great deal more than teaching is required.

Level headedness, Marie Louise von Franz says, and commonsense, self observation and reflection . . . a certain wisdom and humaneness. These sensible attributes are called for because the drama of love is never sensible, but dangerous and alluring; and because the romantic figures and projections originating in our own psyches, always want to seduce us away from reality in to rapture or pull us down into an inner world of fantasy. It's not a matter of refusing love, or passion; on the contrary the task of maturity is to experience it fully, so that we can understand this powerful realm through the capacity of both heart and mind. Whoever cannot surrender to this experience has never lived, she says, whoever founders in it has understood nothing.

So in other words, you don't get anywhere by avoiding love. You have to use it, though, not as a crutch, but as a challenge to develop and strengthen your sense of self. Modjeska quotes the artist Stella Bowen:

Some people believed that . . . happiness was a kind of present that one person could bestow on another. We have to understand that there can be no such thing as belonging to another person (for in the last resort you must be responsible for yourself, just as you must be prepared to die alone). How trite it sounds, how not worth mentioning. But what a discovery it makes.

Later in the book she returns to this theme of being oneself as a necessary prerequisite to loving another:

> What is it we hope to see in the eyes of our lovers?
> What do we want our lovers to see? Our ideal self,
> reflected back in love? A glory we wouldn't recognize as
> our own if we stood alone? Is the cruel truth that we
> seek in love not a loved one but our own heightened
> selves? Narcissus fell into the pond and drowned, drawn
> by the beauty of his own reflection. It was a punishment
> made to fit the crime, for Narcissus, absorbed in himself,
> had never been able to recognize love when it was offered.

So immature lovers (and haven't we all been this) are
really hoping their partner will be not a person at all, just
an admirer, a kind of magic mirror that reflects them
wartless and perfect! When we go out on a 'date' we
naturally are on our best behaviour, smelling sweet. We
hope they'll be impressed. But impressing and presenting
our best can't be the long-term strategy. We have to let
them know us as we are, if we are to avoid being hopelessly mismatched, or sentenced to a lifetime of acting. A
friend of ours took a new girlfriend out on the back of
his motorcycle. All went well, until, parking the bike back
at her apartment, he stumbled and the bike fell over
heavily on the road. Together, laughing, they struggled
to stand it up again. That was when he knew he was
beginning to love her.

Beware of a partner whom you think is just wonderful,
or who thinks you are wonderful. Everyone contemplating
marriage should go on a long and difficult holiday, somewhere without plumbing. Can save a lot of trouble.

But back to *The Orchard*:

We live in a culture that daily encourages us to find our identity in that reflection of another, to experience ourselves as most real when we are in love. We live in a culture that encourages us to see ourselves as others see us.

So we equate ourselves and our value with our beauty, with our bride-price. Hence the obsession with being young and beautiful . . .

The indignity meted out to those women who look to the scalpel and the gym as they cling to youth, is that it can never work. Why would a man who wants a girl (fresh and lovely as girls are) choose a substitute princess? No woman can win that way. And what woman worth her salt wants a man who wants a girl?

What a sentence. 'What woman worth her salt wants a man who wants a girl?' I have always felt this way about breast implants. Surely, big breasts would just attract the kind of man who thinks big breasts are important! The booby prize!

The real point of it all, the deep-down truth, is that youth and beauty are irrelevant. Getting older, getting a deeper knowledge of yourself, and not NEEDING anything from another, finally gets you to the point where love is really possible.

With a shift in the viewing lens from the firmness of the breast to the fullness of being, it may not seem as if everything ends with the arrival of the first lines on our face. On the contrary, it could be that with age, it's all just beginning, for it takes time to come into one's own life, to know one's strength and capacities, to develop the flexibility that allows not the domination of others or ourselves, but a mutuality that trusts those we love with the truth about ourselves.

So does Ettie, for all her tough mindedness, believe in happiness?

> ... there are indeed happy couples, even happy families, but I would say it is not that they are all alike.
>
> When one sees happiness between a man and a woman who have travelled beyond the state of 'being in love' and beyond the war zone, it is blessing to be in their company. Paradoxically it is not so different, this blessing, from the happiness of those who have learned to live full lives without partners, though not necessarily without connections and intimacy (by which I do not – necessarily – mean sex). Happiness is perhaps the wrong word. It is the quality of being fully oneself, not at rest so much as defining one's own terms, not to impose them on others but as a basis of mutual connection – and not only with a spouse. Individuation is closer to the quality I mean, a more hard wrought and painful process than the rose-covered cottage the word happiness conjures up. Though to achieve it, even to begin to achieve it is, surely, a source of the fullest pleasure. It requires the ability to see others as sovereign as oneself; it takes great presence of mind ...

You don't have to be unhappy if your partner is unhappy. Angry if they are angry. Or frightened of their disapproval. You care about them. You care about yourself. You stand on your own ground, and so you can be there fully. It's a lifelong journey to achieve this separateness/closeness thing.

'To see others as sovereign as oneself.' This is what maturity really means.

Extracts from *The Orchard* by Drusilla Modjeska reprinted by permission of Pan Macmillan Australia Pty Ltd. Copyright Drusilla Modjeska 1994.

Further Reading

Arndt, Bettina, *Private Lives*, Penguin, Aust., 1986

Arndt, Bettina, *Taking Sides: Men, Women and the Shifting Social Agenda*, Random House, Aust., 1995

Bass, Ellen & Davis, Laura, *The Courage to Heal: A Guide for Women Survivors of Child Sexual Abuse*, Harper & Row, USA, 1988

Berenson, Bernard G., *Belly to Belly, Back to Back: the Militant Humanism of Robert R. Carkhuff*, Human Resource Development Press, USA, 1975

Berne, Eric, *Games People Play: The Psychology of Human Relationships*, Ballantine Books, USA, 1996

Berne, Eric, *Sex in Human Loving*, Pocket Books, USA 1974

Biddulph, Steve, *Manhood: An Action Plan For Changing Men's Lives*, Finch Publishing, Aust., 1994

Biddulph, Steve & Shaaron, *More Secrets of Happy Children*, HarperCollins, Aust., 1994

Bradshaw, John, *Homecoming: Reclaiming and Championing Your Inner Child*, Bantam Books, USA, 1990

Clarke, Jean Illsley & Dawson, Connie, *Growing Up Again: Parenting Ourselves, Parenting Our Children*, Harper & Row, 1989

Cleese, J., & Skynner, R., *Families and How to Survive Them*, Methuen, UK, 1983

Crenshaw, Dr Theresa L, *Why We Love and Lust: How*

Our Sex Hormones Influence Our Relationships, HarperCollins, 1996

Gottman, John, *Why Marriages Succeed or Fail – and How You Can Make Yours Last,* Bloomsbury, UK, 1997

Harrison, Eric, *Teach Yourself to Meditate,* Simon & Schuster, Aust, 1998 (Perth Meditation Centre, PO Box 1019, Subiaco, WA, 6904)

Henderson, Julie, *The Lover Within: Opening to Energy in Sexual Practice,* Stationhill Press, Barrytown, NY, 1997

Kitzinger, Sheila, *Women's Experience of Sex,* Penguin, UK, 1983

Matthews, Andrew, *Being Happy: A Handbook to Greater Confidence and Security,* Media Masters Pty Ltd, 1988

McClure Goulding, Mary & Goulding, Robert L, *Changing Lives Through Redecision Therapy,* Grove Press, USA, 1979

Modjeska, Drusilla, *The Orchard* (Fiction), Picador, Aust., 1994

Moore, Thomas, *Care of the Soul: A Guide for Cultivating Depth and Sacredness in Everyday Life,* Hodder & Stoughton, 1992

Moore, Thomas, *The Re-enchantment of Everyday Life,* Hodder & Stoughton, 1996

Mullinar, Liz & Hunt, Candida (Eds), *Breaking the Silence: Survivors of Child Abuse Speak Out,* Hodder & Stoughton, 1997

Purves, Libby, *How Not to Be a Perfect Family,* Harper-Collins, UK, 1994

Schnarch, David PhD, *Passionate Marriage: Keeping Love and Intimacy Alive In Committed Relationships,* Owl Books, 1997

Spong, John Shelby, *Living in Sin? A Bishop Rethinks*

Human Sexuality, Harper & Row, USA, 1988

Walsh, Anthony PhD, *The Science of Love: Understanding Love and Its Effects On Mind and Body*, Prometheus Books, 1996

Weir, Bert & Scandrett, Charlie, *You Were Born Special, Beautiful and Wonderful: What Happened?*, Weir Knightsbridge & Assoc., 29 Beatrice St, Bardon, Qld, 4065, 1993

Acknowledgements

Just after the birth of our first child, some close older friends of ours went through a painful marriage break-up. Feeling distressed and helpless, we began a long search to find how it is that some marriages thrive and grow, and others explode into pieces.

Help came from many directions. Some of the ideas in this book, including parts of the Sex–Romance Alliance, The Reconnecting Ritual, and the No-Compromise Route to Fulfilment, were originated by Ken and Elizabeth Mellor. We also greatly benefited from the healing and teaching of Dr Julie Henderson, a leading bioenergetics teacher and practitioner in the US and Australia. Robin Maslen MOA, the father of transactional analysis in Australia, taught us about the Four Cs of couple communication.

Virginia Satir, Bob and Mary Goulding, Colin McKenzie, and many other leaders in the family therapy field had a great effect on our work.

Rex Finch commissioned the first edition, which went into six reprints over twelve years. Publisher Shona Martyn and editor Katie Stackhouse threatened us with another reprint, causing the panic that led to this edition being so significantly revised! John Wright allowed us to use his marvellous cartoons, including some special ones drawn just for the book.

Index

The Complete Secrets
of Happy Children

Steve and Shaaron Biddulph

Together in one edition for the first time, *The Complete Secrets of Happy Children* combines international bestsellers *The Secret of Happy Children* and *More Secrets of Happy Children*.

Steve Biddulph reveals what is really happening in children's minds and what to do about it. With this book you will learn how to let go of old, negative approaches and become a stronger and more loving parent. Together with wife Shaaron, Steve tackles the important concerns of parents today, including:

- How to help toddlers and children feel secure and settled
- How to stop tantrums and whingeing
- Discipline methods that work without hitting or yelling
- Childcare issues and the importance of spending enough time with your child
- Being the best kind of dad
- How to cope if you are a single parent
- Raising sons and raising daughters – their different needs
- Making sure your love gets through

Humorous, easy-to-read, sensible and practical, this books will tell you everything you need to know about raising happy, healthy, confident children, from newborns to teenagers.

Raising Boys

Why Boys are Different – and How to Help Them Become Happy and Well-Balanced Men

Steve Biddulph

In this new edition of the groundbreaking bestseller *Raising Boys*, Steve Biddulph discusses the warm, strong parenting and guidance that boys need.

- How can we teach boys to be happy, confident and kind?
- The three stages of boyhood and how to make them go smoothly
- Testosterone – how it changes behaviour and what to do about it
- How boys' brains are different
- How mothers teach boys about life and love
- The five essentials that fathers provide (and what to do if you're a single mum)
- How to help boys learn a caring attitude to sex
- Eight major changes schools must make to be good places for boys

'A mix of Billy Connolly and Dr Spock ... Steve Biddulph is a publishing phenomenon.' *The Times*

'Steve's advice is really easy to follow – and more importantly, it works.' *BBC Family Life magazine*

Make
www.thorsonselement.com
your online sanctuary

www.thorsonselement.com

thorsons
element